Praise for

WHAT I WAS DOING WHILE YOU WERE BREEDING

"This is a book about so much: Friendship, love, sex, independence, travel, sitcom writing, family, self-destruction, self-confidence. It has it all and you should read it."

—*The Rumpus*

"You should not judge a book by its cover, but luckily this one's as engrossing as its top flap, which I kind of wanted to dive into on sight. There are lots of books out there about being the single girl in your crowd, but Kristin Newman's is a special one; it's truly hilarious and travel-oriented, which makes it perfect for summer."

—*Glamour*

"A memoir of travel and romance—and sex—by a witty TV writer, this is a funny, breezy read for the beach or the plane. Newman has a peppy, sure-footed style, with a sense of self and a passionate curiosity, the most important thing any traveler can have."

—Yahoo, *Armchair Traveler*

"Kristin Newman's tales of wanderlust are at turns hilarious, embarrassing, and then truly inspiring. Her thrilling escapades make me want to get up off the couch and book a ticket to some exotic locale for a sexy adventure of my own. But I probably won't. And neither will you. Just read the book."

—Jane Lynch

"Kristin Newman explodes the idea of the 'singles scene' into a thousand tiny fragments and scatters them globally. This is misspent youth well-spent."

—Patton Oswalt

"I have had the pleasure of joining Kristin on some amazing adventures and can say without question that she is as good a writer as she is a traveler. Which is to say, slightly better when she's had a few glasses of wine."

—Nick Kroll

"If Mark Twain was a woman and he had actually done things in the countries he traveled to, he would have been a lot more pleasant. He also would have written this book instead of *The Innocents Abroad*. This book is so good that, of the many I have blurbed, this is the only one I read."

—Joel Stein, columnist for *Time*, author of
Man Made: A Stupid Quest for Masculinity

"I love my husband and kids, truly I do—but reading *What I Was Doing While You Were Breeding* makes me want to buy a one-way ticket around the world, or rather two tickets—one for me and one for her—so we could party till dawn, flirt with hairy European men, and break several international laws. Kristin puts the 'lust' in wanderlust and makes adventuring and even misadventuring sexy, fun, and, at times, even inspirational."

—Jill Soloway, writer/director *Transparent*

"Since we can't all sit next to Kristin Newman at a dinner party, it's a good thing she wrote *What I Was Doing While You Were Breeding* so we can all enjoy her funny and unexpected tales. Unlike the rest of us, Kristin took the road less traveled and that has made all the difference. Her sparkling wit and adventurous spirit will seduce you just as it did that guy in Argentina . . . and in Russia . . . and in Jordan . . . and so on."

—Nell Scovell, coauthor of *Lean In*

"*What I Was Doing While You Were Breeding* is sly disguised as sexy. It reminded me of George Eliot mixed with a woodshop-safety film. . . . A complete delight."

—Stephen Tobolowsky, actor, author of *The Dangerous Animals Club*

"I wanted to read this book but my wife stole it off my nightstand, laughed at it for three nights straight, and lent it to her friends."

—Rodney Rothman, author of *Early Bird: A Memoir of Premature Retirement*

"Kristin's book is such an uproarious, sidesplitting, jaw-dropping-while-miraculously-somehow-also-self-reflecting page-turner, it makes me feel like I traded in my own wife and children for a time machine and a spot in her globe-trotting duffel bag."

—Rob Kutner, writer for *Conan*, author of *Apocalypse How* and *The Future According to Me*

"Riotously funny, brutally honest, and hopelessly romantic . . . Newman's global romps and brave takedown of the dated, divisive dichotomy between happy breeders and desperate singles is one of the most refreshing things I've read in a long time and proof that everyone has her own path to happily ever after."

—Attica Locke, nationally bestselling author of *The Cutting Season*

What I Was Doing While You Were Breeding

A Memoir

Kristin Newman

Three Rivers Press
New York

Published in the United States by Three Rivers Press,
an imprint of the Crown Publishing Group, a division
of Random House LLC, a Penguin Random House
Company, New York.

www.crownpublishing.com

Three Rivers Press and the Tugboat design are
registered trademarks of Random House LLC.

Library of Congress Cataloging-in-Publication Data is
available upon request.

ISBN 978-0-804-13760-7
eBook ISBN 978-0-8041-3761-4

Printed in the United States of America

Book design by Donna Sinisgalli
Cover design by Jessie Sayward Bright
Cover photography by Martin Westlake/Galley Stock

20 19 18 17 16 15

First Edition

To my mom,

who taught me how to get around an airport,

and throw a great party,

and that "Grown-ups don't just hold hands."

To my dad,

who taught me about balance, in all things,

but especially when hopping across river rocks,

and who says living my life would give him diarrhea.

To my girls,

who let me write about some of their adventures,

and who have been my de facto spouses on mine,

even when they were cheering me on from home.

And to one more person,

but that dedication has to come at the end,

or it'll spoil the whole story…

All things in moderation,

including moderation.

—OSCAR WILDE

Contents

Prologue

....

"I'll Have the House Special"

I am not a slut in the United States of America. I have rarely had a fewer-than-four-night stand in the Land of the Free. I don't kiss married men or guys I work with, I don't text people pictures of my genitalia, I don't go home with boys I meet in bars before they have at least purchased me a couple of meals, I've never shown my boobs for beads. I do not sleep with more than one person at a time, and, sometimes, no more than one per year. In America.

But I really love to travel.

Now, having sex with foreigners is not the only whorish thing I do: I also write sitcoms. For the last fourteen years I've written for shows like *That '70s Show, How I Met Your Mother, Chuck, The Neighbors,* and shows you've never heard of that nonetheless afford me two over-the-top lucky things: the money to buy plane tickets and the time off to travel. What this means about my life is that I spend about nine months a year in a room full of, mostly, poorly dressed men, telling dick jokes and overeating and, sometimes, sitting on the floor with Demi Moore, Ashton Kutcher, and a chimpanzee (before all three found the age difference insurmountable). In the writers' room, we talk a million miles a minute, tearing each other apart for sport and, often, out of love. Sometimes someone makes me cry, and I pretend I'm doing a "bit" where I "run out of the room to cry" even though what I'm really doing is running out of the room to cry. If I'm lucky enough to be fully employed, I get about nine months of this and then a three-month hiatus—unpaid time off from this weird non-corporate grind.

Most days, the writers' room feels like I'm at the most entertaining dinner party in the world. Other times, it feels like I'm at the meanest, longest one. I keep both versions in perspective with my real life's work—running away from home to someplace wonderful. And then, sometimes, having sex there.

Throughout most of my twenties and thirties, in the hiatus months (or years) between shows, I spent between a few weeks and a few months a year traveling. When money was tight, I took road trips with a tent, and when it wasn't, I got on a plane and went as far as I could, to places like China and New Zealand, Jordan and Brazil. To Tibet and Argentina and Australia and most of Europe. To Israel and Colombia and Russia and Iceland. In the beginning, I took these trips with girlfriends, but soon my girls started marrying boys, and then they started making new little girls and boys, and so then I started taking the trips alone. Some of these girls would eventually come back around after a divorce for a trip or two, but then leave me again when they got married for the second time before I'd managed to do it for the first. (When I complained to my friend Hope that she had lapped me in the marriage department, she replied, "I'm not sure the goal is to do it as often as possible." I love her.)

Anyway, everyone around me was engaged in a lot of engaging, marrying, and breeding while I remained resolutely terrified of doing any of it. I did want to have a family *someday* . . . it was just that "someday" never seemed to feel like "today." I wanted love, but I also wanted freedom and adventure, and those two desires fought like angry obese sumo wrestlers in the dojo of my soul. That wrestling match threatened to body-slam me into a veritable Bridget-Jonesian-sad-girl singlehood, which I was resolutely against, both personally and as an archetype. And so to ward that off, I kept moving.

Pretty early on in my travel career I discovered two vital things. First, that I'm someone a little different on the road, and that vacation from being my home self feels like a great sleep after a long day. Second, that you can have both love *and* freedom when you fall in love with an exotic local in an exotic locale, since there is a return ticket next to the bed that you by law will eventually have to use. These sweet, sexy, epic little vacationships became part of my identity—I was The Girl with the Great International Romance Stories at dinner parties, and around the writers' room table. And I began to need my trips like other people need religion.

But my mom will be pleased to hear that my addiction

to sexy people in sexy places really grew out of a nonsexual obsession: I love to do the thing you're supposed to do in the place you're supposed to do it. That means *always* getting the specialty of the house. That means smoking cigarettes I don't smoke at the perfect corner café for hours at a time in Paris, and stripping naked for group hot-tubbing with people you don't want to see naked in Big Sur. It means riding short, fuzzy horses that will throw me onto the arctic tundra in Iceland, or getting beaten with hot, wet branches by old naked women in stifling *banyas* in Moscow. When these moments happen, I get absurdly happy, like the kind of happy other people report experiencing during the birth of their children. And getting romanced by a Brazilian in Brazil, or a Cretan in Crete . . . this, to me, just happens to be the gold medal in the Do the Thing You're Supposed to Do Olympics.

I love that I am but one of millions of single girls hitting the road by themselves these days. A hateful little ex-boyfriend once said that a house full of cats used to be the sign of a terminally single woman, but now it's a house full of souvenirs acquired on foreign adventures. He said it derogatorily: *Look at all of this tragic overcompensating in the form of tribal masks and rain sticks.* But I say that plane tickets replacing cats might be the best evidence of women's progress as a gender. I'm damn proud of us.

Also, since I have both a cat and a lot of foreign souvenirs, I broke up with that dude and went on a really great trip.

1

"Drugs Make You a Better Person"

Los Angeles International → Paris Charles de Gaulle
→ Amsterdam Schiphol
Departing: March 24, 2000

The first time I blew off steam internationally was not born of carpe diem. It was born of deep despair.

I was twenty-six, and I traveled to Europe with my childhood friend Hope on a "girls' trip" in the wake of a breakup with my first and most consequential love, Vito. (This is obviously not his name. I let him name himself, though, so, for our purposes, I had a six-year relationship with a man named Vito.) I handled the heartbreak like many twenty-six-year-olds handled big breakups at the beginning of the third millennium: I pierced my belly button, got a Meg Ryan–circa–*French Kiss*–style bleach job and haircut, and went to Amsterdam.

First, a little more on the man behind the body-reclaiming piercing: Vito and I met our freshman year of college, had a close friendship sprinkled with drunken make-outs and missed connections for two years, then finally fell madly in love in the way it turns out you only fall in love when you're twenty and doing it for the first time. (It took me fifteen years of unsuccessfully chasing that first high to understand that. Slow learner.)

We fell in love in the early nineties, and so Vito and I thought a lot of Ethan Hawke and Winona Ryder movies were *about us*. (Also Ethan Hawke and Julie Delpy movies. Vito had a goatee and hated The Man, so basically anything with Ethan Hawke.) After graduation, we laughed at our friends who went straight to work at ad agencies and consulting firms, and instead backpacked around Europe for the summer, then spent a dreamy fall, winter, and spring working and skiing in Vail, Colorado. In Vail, we sublet a room from two racist brothers who talked a lot about their Scottish ancestry, and who were trying to become "alpine models."

"You just gotta be a rad skier and be super good-looking, and I really think my skiing's there this year," the younger racist explained.

After Vail, Vito got into grad school at UC Santa Barbara, and I moved to L.A. to try to write for television. It turned out that meant spending eighty hours a week driving around town with carloads of film and fetching coffee for writers. It meant squeezing in time to work on my own writing, only to have a male writer notice and say, "Awwww, you're writing something? That's so cute!" It meant spending lunch hours giving a high-level writer ideas for his script that he jotted down word for word, getting more hopeful and proud with each "Great idea!" he gave me, and then being told over the check, "Someday you're going to make a great producer's wife." It meant pitching jokes in a writers' room and hearing, "Aw, isn't she pretty?" before being told to pitch it again while doing jumping jacks or, perhaps, sitting on the showrunner's lap. It meant always, always laughing all of it off.

Anyway, while I navigated the world of Hollywood, Vito moved to jasmine-scented Santa Barbara to learn how to surf, and became a part-time forest ranger and environmental studies grad student who couldn't wrap his head around ever living in Los Angeles, where TV writers have to live. For the next three years we commuted the hundred miles between Los Angeles and Santa Barbara to see each other, and I tried to think of something else to do with my life. I racked my brain—it certainly wasn't like long hours of drudgery and sexual harassment were so satisfying that they seemed worth losing the love of my life over. But, despite the massive motivation to come up with an alternate life plan, I couldn't think of anything else I wanted to do. And, eventually, I realized that meant something.

So Vito and I spent our early twenties planning our retirement. Really. There was no version of the next thirty years that enabled us to both get the lives we wanted and be together, so we just skipped to the part on which we agreed: retiring on an avocado ranch in wine country with a lot of Saint Bernards somewhere around 2035.

But ignoring the reality of the here and now didn't last, and that's when the relationship, as Vito said, "became about talking about the relationship." We went to couples' counseling at twenty-four, weeping to what must have been a highly amused therapist about our enormous troubles.

"I just don't picture myself as the *type* of person who lives in L.A. Plus, it kills me how much fossil fuel we're burning by driving back and forth every week," my tortured environmentalist would say to the therapist and me.

"Do we *seriously* have to add fossil fuels to our list of problems?!" I would wail.

"I'm just saying, it really bothers me."

The therapist would pause. "So ... you spend three nights a week together, and Kristin lives in Santa Barbara full-time for three months in the spring," she would say, trying to paint us the ridiculous picture she was seeing. "That would work fine for some people. Do you think there is something about identifying this as a 'problem' that is working for you?"

We scoffed at this. But, years later, I would realize it was the truest thing any therapist has ever said to me. Coloring Vito as ultimately unavailable, all six years that he spent telling me he wanted to be with me forever, *worked for me*. It made it easy as pie to be 100 percent sure about him. I would learn from many subsequent *available* men that that is probably how Vito and I lasted six years.

But I wouldn't learn that for a *long* time. And hence we have this book.

The struggle finally broke us, and Vito and I ended it all one day after Y2K didn't happen in Santa Barbara. We wept and hugged and said we'd love each other forever, and then he put me on a train to Los Angeles, and I spent the entire ride back crying, knowing that he was The One and that no one would ever understand or love me the way he had ever again. I hoped that he was racing along the road next to me in his car, and would be waiting for me at the train station in the Burbank night. But I got off the train, and the station was empty.

A couple of months later, a girls' trip presented itself.

Hope and I met on the first day of eighth grade, when we were both new kids at the same school, and so huddled together for warmth in the chilly waters of junior high. We stayed friends when I went to Northwestern, to go to football games and gain a lot of beer and pizza weight, and she went to the University of Oregon, to ride her bike in the rain and lose a lot of drug weight. By the end of college, it looked like I had eaten her. Hope, however, could always keep a lot of balls in the air, so still managed to spend a semester studying abroad in Ecuador, and graduated with a double major in business and Spanish in four years, while some of her fellow college buddies ended up living in boxes in San Francisco. By twenty-six she had grown into an adventurous, sporty, constantly cheerful woman who worked hard and played hard, so when she invited me to tag along on a business trip to Amsterdam for some girl fun she said I desperately needed, it was easy to say yes.

After four years of assistant work on a variety of television shows, I had just been offered my first writing job, on

That '70s Show, beginning the following June. That miracle meant there was a date on the horizon when I could start to pay off my credit cards. (Four years of assistant pay had led to debt caused by splurges on things like socks and groceries.) So I bought a plane ticket—girl fun, here I come! Then Hope invited her boyfriend to come along.

"You don't mind, right?"

I minded. Feeling like I'd be a third wheel, I tried to bow out, which is when Hope's boyfriend decided to fix it all by inviting his best friend.

"Oh, God, not Mike!" Hope and I both protested.

But Mike, a very sweet, short drug addict and high school dropout with blue hair, pink skin, rodent-like eyes, and a prison record, was *in*.

"Ahhhh, sounds pretty cozy," Mike's friends would say to me knowingly. "I think Mike's about to help you get over your breakup!"

"Mm," I'd reply, as Hope peeked at me apologetically over her adult beverage.

We started our trip in Paris, where Mike provided us with scintillating commentary during our cultural tour of the city's landmarks, like Notre Dame:

"So this place is so famous they named a school after it!"

. . . and the Louvre:

"What's the Louvre?"

. . . and European ambulances:

"They sound different!"

We were all piled into one room in an ancient, crumbling hotel on a little park on the Seine, directly across from Notre Dame. At like thirty dollars a night, with a view of the cathedral, it had to be the crummiest hotel in the best location in the world, and I had stayed there four years earlier on my postcollege summer trip with Vito. The place *sang* with memories of my first trip to Europe with my first love, and so my mood was not particularly *en rose*.

Because of my dark cloud, and the fact that I hadn't kissed anyone besides my ex in six years, the idea of a "palate-cleansing hookup" was oft suggested by my travel companions.

"A sex sorbet!" Hope clarified.

"What's sorbet?" Mike asked.

It made me feel like Vito and I were breaking up all over again to even picture such a thing, but sex sorbets did always seem to make people feel better in movies. So I put on a little ditty one night, and we headed out to find some fun.

We found a lot to drink. And a big, hot Australian bartender who invited us back to his friend's groovy, velvet-filled apartment, late at night, for what turned out to be an extraordinary amount of hash. Things were looking good for the bartender and me as I threw back drinks at the rate you do when you are trying to flirt for the first time in six years ... And then I don't remember anything else besides waking up the next morning in our little room on the Seine.

"The bartender helped us carry you down the four flights of stairs," Hope told me. "He was very sweet."

So, my palate was still not cleansed. It tasted like wine and bile, in fact. But the trip was not over.

After a few days with Hope and the boys, I decided to spend a little extra time in Paris, and sent them on to Amsterdam without me. Because I needed a break from Mike, but also because I wanted to be the girl who hung out alone in Paris. You see, over the years, Vito and I had fought many times over conversations like this one:

"I want to go to Hawaii for my spring break," he might say.

"I have to work that week," I'd reply.

"Okay, I guess I'll just go on my own," Vito would decide.

And then he would.

Now, 2013 Kristin would find this to be a completely reasonable thing to do. 2013 Kristin would do exactly the same thing, and would love that she was with a guy who could head off on a solo adventure as well as she could. But, *boy*, did 1998 Kristin feel differently. I had no urge to go on trips without Vito. I wanted to spend every spare minute with him. I would drive as fast as I could up to Santa Barbara to see him the first moment I could, refusing to stop even when I needed to pee and my car was running on gas fumes. Vito, on the other hand, was closer to where I am today—thrilled when I could come along on adventures, but excited about going alone, too.

Which made me furious.

I wanted to be the girl who could have fun alone in

Paris. It scared me a little, but I remembered the lesson my mom taught me at age seven in a swimming pool in Hawaii. I was a shy little girl and an only child, so on vacations I was usually playing alone, too afraid to go up to the happy groups of kids and introduce myself. Finally, on one vacation, my mom asked me which I'd rather have: a vacation with no friends, or *one scary moment*. So I gathered up all of my courage, and swam over to the kids, and there was *one scary moment* . . . and then I had friends for the first time on vacation. After that, one scary moment became something I was always willing to have in exchange for the possible payoff. I became a girl who knew how to take a deep breath, suck it up, and walk into any room by herself.

So I took a deep breath, put my three travel companions on the train to Amsterdam, and settled into my first time alone in a foreign city.

It didn't go all that well.

I kept getting on the train in the wrong direction, and finding myself in restaurants without a book. (It's almost impossible to have a meal alone without something to read. Try it. It's terrible.) There is no time or place in Paris where a woman is safe from unwanted advances from a Frenchman. I was constantly followed by creepy men in the streets, and a man in a turtleneck (harmless, but ick) approached me in a park at ten in the morning, and asked if I wanted to become his lover. I was nervous and lonely, and wrote Vito postcards from cafés we had visited together, furious that I was nervous and lonely. Vito would have had a great time in Paris alone for two days. I needed to figure my shit out.

And that was how I found myself walking by the bar where the cute Australian bartender worked. I had never gone into a bar by myself before, but I decided to "drop in" for a drink. *Oh my God, I was just walking by and here's your bar! Paris is such a small town!* The Australian was very sweet, and laughed off my poor reaction to the hash the night before, and poured me a beer. And then another one. And then even one more. I just kept sitting there, feeling awkward but needing a win, and not knowing where else I could find one.

At the end of the night, the bartender closed down the bar, and put me in a cab. *Strike.*

So, feeling like a bit of a failure, but proud of myself for trying, I got on a train going in the right direction and went to Amsterdam.

It turned out that while Mike might not have been the ideal travel companion for a cultural tour of Paris, he was just the ticket in Amsterdam. You know how beautiful it is to watch someone in his element? LeBron James playing basketball, Pavarotti singing, Ryan Gosling breathing? Taking Mike from Paris to Amsterdam was like watching an elephant seal flopping around on the sand, dragging its monstrous, awkward body inch by painful inch across the land until it reaches the sea, slips into the water ... and glides off in one majestic *swoosh*, jumping and diving gracefully effortlessly.

We had been in our first bar in Amsterdam for thirty

seconds when Mike pointed at someone in the back, and said:

"That guy."

Was Mike taller than he had been in Paris? I found myself thinking. He made a beeline through the thousands of people who had not caught his eye, up to a thin, average-looking, twentysomething dude we came to know as Peter the Dutch Drug Dealer. Peter the Dutch Drug Dealer gave us a napkin on which was written a list of bars and clubs where he could be found at various hours of the day. All twenty-four hours were accounted for, so apparently his wares were good enough to eliminate the need for sleep. He had a friend with him, a black prostitute named Victoria, who was wearing a dress of a length such that passersby could see her three labia hoops dangle when she walked. Later in the week we watched Victoria climb onto a table at a club, insert her ring-clad fingers into the mysterious place from whence those hoops dangled, and then remove her fingers . . . now stripped of jewelry. I believe this happened at around eight on a Tuesday morning.

But back to less seedy topics—drugs. After a moment of discussion, Peter the Dutch Drug Dealer handed Mike a little baggie of treats, which we spent the next week watching Mike smoke, or swallow, or snort. Then, after watching to see how our human guinea pig would react, we would make our decisions about whether or not to follow.

Now, I was twenty-six, but before this trip, my experiences with drugs had been limited to a rare sleep-inducing joint, and one crazy day of mushrooms at Northwestern where I raced armadillos and learned what love was. One of my dad's best pieces of parenting advice had been very simple: *wait*. He didn't tell me to abstain from sex and drugs forever, which I'm sure would have made me try everything immediately. He just told me to take a beat, watch my friends try things out, learn what to do and what not to do based on their mistakes and triumphs, and then try out what I was going to try.

Without consciously deciding to, I took that advice to heart in many elements of my life: *just wait*. With marriage and children, but also with drugs and men. I was a social drinker, but had skipped the normal youthful drug experimentation in which most of my single friends had participated. I had a boyfriend. Vito and I cooked dinner, and went to farmer's markets, and, when we were feeling crazy, made fondue. We had visited Amsterdam during our postcollege summer of backpacking, but had mostly indulged in handfuls of Dutch pancakes that you could get to go in adorably wrapped tin-foil packages. Sure, we had smoked a little pot, but usually during the day, while riding bikes along the dykes, or dangling our feet into what we thought was the North Sea (it wasn't) and singing "(Sittin' On) The Dock of the Bay" more times than sober people might have. We hadn't immersed ourselves in the dark underbelly of Amsterdam.

But now I had a friend named Peter the Dutch Drug Dealer.

Hope, her boyfriend, Blue-Haired Mike, and I had planned on staying in Amsterdam for three days, before heading out to see the outrageous color of Holland's spring tulip fields on our way to the Hague, where we would learn about international tribunals. Instead, we got stuck in Amsterdam for a long, dark week, in a world where we saw the sun for about forty-five minutes per day, usually in the late morning, during the journey from the back door of a club to our blackout-curtained hotel room. Mothers would be bicycling their children across the charming bridges of Amsterdam on their way to school when we were dragging ourselves home, shaky and exhausted and hours from being able to sleep.

I should be clear that, throughout this revelry, I was still in deep, dark, brokenhearted pain. Even Mike was irritated with the amount I was talking about the loss of my first love, and his body should have been drugged past the ability to feel irritation (or surgery). But even he grew weary of how much I needed to talk about whether I had done the right thing a few weeks earlier, when I turned down my very first marriage proposal.

The proposal came six weeks after Vito and I broke up, and one week after I checked his voicemail (I know) and heard a message from a girl who turned out to be a freshman student he had just started fucking. I was heartbroken and lonelier than I'd ever been in my life when Vito showed up on my doorstep with roses and asked me to marry him.

A few years earlier, in a panic about the many bikini-clad undergrads with whom a UC Santa Barbara grad student spends his time, I had broken down and read Vito's journal. (I know.) In it he said that, in two years, after he got his master's degree, he was going to propose to me. Great news, right? No stories of deflowering teenaged surfer girls! Sadly, I did not see it that way.

Despite how desperately I loved him, I panicked. To me, marriage was an ending, not a beginning. A stone on my chest. A giving-up, a decision to walk away from an interesting life for one just like everyone else's. Much more "ever after" than "happily." Why did it feel that way? Well . . . I'll get to that later.

After reading Vito's journal, I made sure to mention to him early and often that marriage was not for me. I talked about how I wanted to spend my life with him, since a life without him felt like a life without my favorite limb. I said that I wanted to someday waaaaaaay down the line have kids, but that marriage was for *other* people. Conventional people. People who overpaid for T-shirts when babies were starving, people who worried about whether or not their artwork matched their sofas. People who had to put some weird legal stamp on something we already had.

"Why do people need to put some weird legal stamp on something we already have?" Vito eventually started saying, too.

So when he proposed six weeks after our breakup, I knew he didn't actually want to be married to me and living in Los Angeles—he just wanted to jump in his car, drive too fast to get to me like at the end of a movie, and alleviate our suffering. (And make up for sleeping with his freshman student.) But the problem had never been our commitment to each other—it was the fact that we wanted to live different lives. So I said no, and he didn't seem surprised or particularly upset.

"Consider it a standing offer!" he said cheerfully, before getting back into his car.

And then he drove back to Santa Barbara, and soon went back to the nineteen-year-old student whom he had started seeing about five minutes after we broke up. Meanwhile, I spent a few months in both a metaphorical and literal fetal position, and wondered, like so many ex-girlfriends of forest rangers before me, if I would ever be able to use the tent he gave me for Valentine's Day again.

I was *really* sad about it all. And that's why one night in Amsterdam, Mike gave me Ecstasy.

That's not really true. Mike gave me Ecstasy because the four of us could barely stand each other. Hope was mad at her boyfriend for going to a sex show without her. (The tip-off was the ten fingernail scratch marks down his chest. Audience participation. The boys were subsequently kicked out of Hope's free hotel room.) Mike was mad at me because Hope's boyfriend tattled that I stayed behind in Paris because I wanted a break from Mike's asinine questions. Hope's boyfriend was mad at me for being a snob about his friend. I was mad at Hope for being a crying, angry mess all as a result of bringing two stupid boys on our girl trip. And we had another week to go.

"We need a chemical bridge back to friendship," Mike reasoned.

And, because the subject was drugs, he was right. *Damn,* look at that seal swim! So we all thought for a moment about how little we wanted to spend another week with the people around us, and then reached for the bag of pills.

Several months later, Mike admitted that he had found this bag of pills on the floor of the biggest coffee shop in Amsterdam, the place at the top of the *Let's Go Europe* list of big, college-kid drug bars. And that he wasn't absolutely sure that what was inside the bag was Ecstasy, and not, say, the kind of poison that isn't really, really fun.

It wasn't that other kind of poison. It was *really* fun. *So* much fun! We all loved each other again! Amsterdam wasn't sad and dirty, it was filled with light and joy! Hope's boyfriend and I shared a transcendent dance moment to "Bésame Mucho," our bodies attracting an audience with a perfect merengue I still think about. I saw Mike's sweet heart for all of its sweet sweetness, and my judgmental nature dropped away as I floated out of my judgmentally judging skin, finally understanding that drugs make you a better person. Hope and I cried on each other out of joy for our lifelong friendship. And, somewhere in some bar in Amsterdam, we met Fiona, the twenty-year-old doughy British girl on crutches who wanted to make out with me.

So I grew up just a couple of years before the generations of girls who all kiss other girls and like it. When I was in college, Katy Perry was a toddler in a romper and knee socks, decades away from being a grown woman in a romper and knee socks. A social scientist might argue that the girl-on-girl trend started with rave culture . . . and Ecstasy. Which is an argument that can certainly be supported by my very first experience with raves and Ecstasy.

Now, if taking pills and then having one's first lesbian

experience with a crippled British girl isn't the thing to do in Amsterdam, I just don't know what is. I'd never been hit on by a woman before, probably because I'd never beamed love in all directions simultaneously before. But that night Fiona (like everyone) got hit in the face with a big handful of Kristin love, and so zeroed in.

We sat together for a long time, talking as closely and intensely as only two people on hard drugs can, and I started to realize that *this woman was flirting with me!* And . . . was I flirting back? As I watched our nose-to-nose conversation from somewhere above and to the left of my own body, I wondered if I would have the courage to do something so *dirty*, so *experimental*, in front of people who would bring the story home with us.

Ultimately, it was the intense talking and sharing that was the undoing of Fiona. She shared with me that she had had more than thirty sexual partners in her twenty years. Since, at twenty-six, my sex number was three, this caused me to see little cartoon STDs float around her head, like pink hearts that might go *pop pop pop* around a cartoon character in love. And while I thought Fiona's pierced tongue seemed like a good addition to what might be my only lesbian sex experience (lesbian sex being so tongue-reliant and all), she really was so very *doughy*. And that sticky, shiny, clammy sheen on her face, that wondrous thing I like to call "drug sweat" . . . that didn't bode well for what I might find elsewhere. And there were the crutches, and the broken ankle that she couldn't remember how she broke, which seemed unwieldy in a naked wrestling scenario (which was basically what I gathered lesbian sex was). Plus, for the rest of my life, *Mike*, of all people, would have a ridiculous story to tell about me. But, at the end of the night, I just felt like too many people before me had decided Fiona was The Thing to Do in the Place You're Supposed to Do It. She was probably crippled from it.

And so Mike slept with her instead.

I put my foot down after a week of the dark side, and dragged everyone out of bed at the crack of three p.m. for some sight-seeing. We went to Anne Frank's house, and then for pancakes (sweet). We went to the Van Gogh museum, and then for pancakes (savory). And, one day, I forced everybody onto the train, and out to see the tulip fields.

We chugged instant train coffee and stared out the windows at the Dutch farmland, which looked like it had been colored by a giant kindergartener. Miles of red next to miles of pink next to miles of purple next to miles of yellow. Mike's blue hair framed by all of those colors made him look like a character in *Charlie and the Chocolate Factory*. The goodwill from the drugs that had opened my mind and heart to all of humanity was still lingering, and it made me tolerant and peaceful when Mike asked stupid questions. Hope's head was on her boyfriend's shoulder, all forgiven there, too. In two years they would be married, and in five they would be divorced . . . because he still hadn't grown out of raves and drugs.

I would go home feeling like I had had a real adventure, on my own, without a boyfriend. I'd learned that getting on a plane could make me feel better, and that, regardless of how it had gone, I was the kind of girl who sometimes hung out alone in Paris. The kind of girl who took Ecstasy and knew a guy named Peter the Dutch Drug Dealer and could have made out with a crippled British girl. And that was the first thing that made me feel better about the death of the life I thought I was going to live with Vito. There was a new life coming, and it was going to be as colorful as Dutch tulip fields.

In two months I would start dating my friend Trevor, who would help me get over my first heartbreak, and whose heart I would break two years later when I realized at twenty-nine that I desperately needed to be single for the first time in my life. But, in that moment, the sun was shining, and we were four friends traveling by train through Holland in the spring. I hadn't had my international sex sorbet, and I hadn't kissed a girl, but I had gotten out of my heartbroken fetal position and taken a trip across an ocean. And I liked it.

2

"If I Don't
Sleep with
This Russian
Bartender,
the Terrorists
Win"

Los Angeles International → Moscow Sheremetyevo
Departing: May 7, 2002

I used 9/11 to rationalize cheating. I'm not proud of it, but it's important that you know. And I'd like you to read the following story through a nine-months-after-9/11 lens. Remember that time? We were all a little more grateful for life, a little less sure of the future? Right? Remember?

Yeah, I know, it just sucked. But unfortunately my first actual success at a vacation romance was also my first (and only) time cheating.

It was on a trip to Russia two years into my relationship with Trevor, to whom I now offer a heartfelt apology. Trevor and I had been friends for years while I was dating Vito, and then, six months after Vito and I broke up, Trevor asked me on a date. He was a cheerful curmudgeon who hated most people, so I took it as a great compliment that he liked me. After two years, we were living together, and he really wanted to get married. As usual, I did not.

I was about to turn twenty-nine, *Sex and the City* was at its peak, and I didn't really understand a word of it. I'd never been single as an adult. I couldn't speak with Carrie-like authority about the difference between twenty- and thirtysomething men, I couldn't entertain a dinner party with stories of ridiculous things I'd done to find love. I'd never had bad dates, or good dates. Really, I'd never had any dates, because my last decade had been spent in two almost back-to-back relationships with guys who had first been close friends of mine. In both cases, we'd gotten drunk one night, kissed, said "I love you," and then been together for several years.

So I was starting to wonder if I'd just never have crazy single-girl stories. Which felt like I was choosing to skip a vital life experience, like seeing Paris or having a child, the memory of which would comfort and entertain me as I lay in my old-lady bed, knowing that I had *really done it.*

Trevor was handsome and hilarious and weird in a way I loved. But he was also an aspiring comedy writer who, like all aspiring comedy writers, was regularly unemployed. The same month we started dating, I had finally stopped aspiring and started doing, getting my first writing job on *That '70s Show,* and so his unemployment was also accompanied by depression since, every morning, I went off to his dream job. This was a big bummer for both of us. I loved him, and he moved in with me when his lease was up during a period of unemployment, but I didn't plan on marrying him. I didn't think being in a relationship with someone I didn't want to marry was a problem, mostly because, as I've said, I had never really wanted to *get* married, *period.*

So why was that? Most everyone says your feelings about marriage come from your parents' marriage. I don't know if that's the whole explanation, but here is my parents' story, which definitely had at least some influence:

My parents met when they were young, tan, blond Southern California lifeguards at the same pool in 1967. Picture everyone in *Gidget,* and you get the idea. They got married very fast and very young, at barely twenty and twenty-four, and I grew up experiencing them as very much in love—with me, and with each other. They showered together, they danced in the kitchen, they locked the bedroom door on Saturday mornings.

But after eighteen years, they had grown dramatically apart. The nineteen-year-old lifeguard whom my father had married had turned into a workaholic international corporate lawyer, whose world was getting bigger with every year. The young, beautiful sailor and naval officer who whisked my mother off as a new bride to live in Newport, Rhode Island, and Naples, Italy, had turned into a juvenile probation officer who worked nine to five (which was considered part-time in our house) and who was a cheerful homebody, happiest on the couch with me, my mom, and a box of wine.

He resented the housekeeper my mother hired so she didn't have to spend her few free hours cleaning the house. She resented that she was working constantly to bring home a big check that she wanted to use to see the world, and yet he insisted on going to the same condo in Maui year after year, where we would make sandwiches and break into the beachfront pool down the road. She would buy him flying lessons for his birthday, because as a young man he had dreamed of being a pilot, and he would feel criticized for not being enough for her. She wanted him to have a life about more than us, he wanted her to have a life that was more about us.

It broke.

Following are the lessons I internalized about marriage as a result of my parents' marriage:

1. Getting married young is gambling on a game you don't know how to play. You don't know who either of you is going to become. If you get married before you are fully cooked, you have no idea if you are marrying someone who will ultimately be compatible with you.

2. Marriage is a limiter. It limits your freedom, and it limits your capacity to follow your dreams. If you do make the mistake of growing while married, your marriage will end.

3. No matter how in love you start out, no matter how much you dance in the kitchen and lock the

bedroom door on Saturday mornings, love will die.

And so when people like Vito and Trevor asked me to marry them, I said no.

My best friend, Sasha, was mystified about why I would be spending what she called my "high-worth years" with someone I wasn't going to marry. The world was my oyster, *now*, she would say, but it wouldn't be that way forever. I found this ridiculous. I wanted to have kids eventually, so I knew I'd get married someday. But not yet, not by a long shot. When I was a kid, I told my mom I wanted to have babies when I was as old as possible. Men got married and had babies late into their thirties and forties; I certainly could do the same.

But this was a decade before I noticed something important: *Those older men were usually not marrying women who were also in their thirties and forties.* Ten years later, I would watch the men my age dating women much younger than they were *because those women still had time to slowly date and enjoy before they had to have babies.* Somehow, despite everyone telling me this was how it was going to work, I was sure it wouldn't for me. When *I* was in my twenties and older guys would ask me out, I thought they were creepy, and unattractive, and way too old. It never occurred to me that I was the only twentysomething woman who found thirtysomething successful men creepy.

"Why do you think you hate men with jobs?" Sasha would ask.

Anyway, there I was, living with a depressed, unemployed man whom I loved but was not going to marry, when Sasha invited me on a trip to Russia. Sasha was living on the East Coast, and so for years we had been taking annual girl trips to see each other. The Russia trip happened because Sasha was born in Moscow, and immigrated to the U.S. when she was three. When I met her on the first day of fifth grade, I took one look at the little girl with the uneven bowl haircut given to her by her frugal Russian father and thought, *That is the cutest boy in school.*

But Sasha was now a beautiful twenty-nine-year-old woman with an expensive haircut, and had spent the last two years mixing and sleeping with princes of industry and children of world leaders at Yale Law School. Nothing made Sasha calmer than going to Neiman Marcus, because it felt like the farthest place from the smell of stewed cabbage in her childhood home. She taught me about expensive shoes before either of us could afford expensive shoes, and we chipped in together on one pair of "time-share" Manolos that we shipped back and forth between Los Angeles and New Haven for special occasions, or planned run-ins with exes.

Sasha's mother suggested they take a trip back to Russia, their first time back since they fled to give Sasha a better life twenty-six years earlier. I jumped on the chance to travel to Russia with Russians (the thing to do in the place, etc.) and off we went.

On the plane, Sasha sat next to a barrel-bellied, middle-aged man from Phoenix named Tommy. He was heading to Russia to pick up his pregnant mail-order bride. Tommy pulled out photos. She was eighteen, and spectacularly beautiful. He had met her a few months prior, when, after e-mailing with several women, he traveled to Russia to see which one he liked. The way it worked was this: the girls were put up in different rooms in the same hotel. He visited each girl with a translator, sort of taking her out for a test drive. He picked the one he liked, and spent a couple of weeks with her. She got pregnant, and so now he was going to bring her to her new life in America, where she would be a new mommy to Tommy's two fat children from his first marriage, and would receive a tract home and a new red Buick convertible. He had pictures of the car and the fat kids and the tract home with him, too.

"Have you learned any Russian?" Sasha asked him.

"Oh, no, she'd rather learn English, I'm sure," Tommy replied. "All she wants is to be American."

Sasha squeezed her mother's hand.

For a few weeks we had been practicing "speaking Russian." This did not mean actually speaking Russian, it just meant speaking English with a Russian attitude; i.e., dramatic and full of impending doom. My guidebook told me that the national anthem for Ukraine translated roughly to "We have not yet died!" That was the most victorious and optimistic version they could come up with. When Russians meet, their "Nice to meet you" literally translates to "How many years, how many winters?" Why couldn't it at least be summers? It's all very dramatic and dark in Russia.

So when we were "practicing Russian," Sasha and I would translate "Enjoy your meal" into "I hope you don't choke and leave your family devastated." "Have a nice day" became "Today, try to forget this world is gray and bleak."

Et cetera.

Sasha did teach me a couple of actual Russian phrases that became my party trick for the next three weeks. I could say "I am a bride for sale" with a pretty decent accent. Also "Be my daddy" and "American thighs." When not chirping those phrases, though, I was just the chesty blond girl smiling and nodding while Sasha chatted up Russians. I reminded myself of Ulla, the agreeable but only Swedish-speaking secretary in Mel Brooks's *The Producers*. I'd smile, nod, smile, nod, then Sasha would turn to me and say:

"Kristin, say your thing!"

"I am a bride for sale!" Ulla would proudly pipe up.

And we would have new Russian friends.

I did ask Sasha's mother how to say "Have a nice day" in Russian, but she just frowned and said, "We don't really say that."

The trip was a combination Russian history tour and walk down Sasha's mother's memory lane. We met the original Sasha after whom my Sasha had been named, and had big dinner parties full of her mother's old Russian friends and the families they'd formed in the twenty-six years since she'd last seen them. No one spoke English, and Sasha and her mother both spoke Russian, so at these dinners I would have to sit quietly and pick at my egg, cheese, and mayonnaise bowl that Russians call a "salad."

Sitting quietly at dinner parties was not my natural strong suit. At home, I worked *hard* at dinner parties. Not just at being entertaining, which I believe to be a holy duty of dinner party guests, but also at keeping the conversation constantly going, noticing people who were being left out and asking questions to draw them in, filling the awkward silences. Maybe this need to keep everyone happy and getting along is just my nature, or maybe it stems from a childhood as an only child of a disintegrating marriage, trying to be the happy glue that kept the splintering family together. Either way, I'm not complaining, since it's a skill that's probably exclusively responsible for my success as a sitcom writer.

Sitcom writers often group write, sitting around a big table, so we talk all day long. Sometimes, on some shows, you literally never sit alone in front of a computer just writing. And I worked exactly as hard in a writers' room, around that table, as I did around dinner tables. I never realized how hard I worked around tables day and night until the trip to Russia, when I couldn't. I just had to *sit there*. At first this was *excruciating*. I felt completely not myself, dead weight in a little life raft adrift in a sea of incomprehensible and sometimes stilted conversation.

Earlier that year, at a meditation workshop with a stressed-out friend, the meditation guide was walking us through an exercise, and asked us a question that we were to think about as we sat.

"With no thoughts, with no words, what am I?"

Dead. Immediately, with medium-size panic and a shortness of breath, that was my answer. Without thoughts, words, *speech* . . . death. My career and my identity were filled with millions of words daily, and without them I would be a black hole. My friend and I talked about the question after the class, and I was surprised to hear that her reaction had been absolutely opposite from mine. For her, the idea of no words, and no thoughts, made her deeply calm and peaceful.

For me it meant I was gone.

But on that trip to Russia, I eventually got used to being without words. I could still smile at people, and pass the bread, and look friendly. I was not just the words that came out of my mouth. I was still there without them. And that's when I just ate my cheese salad and *relaxed*. I relaxed to such a degree that I realized I had never been relaxed at any dinner party in my entire life. This was my favorite part about my trip to Russia.

Aside from Aleg.

My Russian lover was a bartender. You will find that bartenders will become a recurring theme. Eventually, in my early thirties, I made a decision: no more dating people who serve food or drink in the United States (excluding Hawaii and Alaska). Now, foodservers of these United States, don't get offended. If I lived anywhere else, I would love to take you out for a drink. But I live in Los Angeles, and so dating a waiter or bartender here means you are *actually* dating an actor or model or musician, which is an unreasonable, self-destructive thing to do.

But a no-bartenders rule is just as unreasonable when traveling abroad. Especially when you're traveling alone, since there's often no one to talk to but the people who are serving you. Which brings us back to Aleg, and his sharp, exquisite Russian features, his floppy, shiny, dark hair, his deep, tortured Russian eyes. I met him one night when Sasha and I went to his bar for a drink, where I looked into those eyes and cooed, *"Vodka tonica,"* which is Russian for "vodka tonic." I said it with a great accent. Then we took our drinks and found a table. But Aleg and I couldn't stop staring at each other.

"I love him," was all I could say to Sasha. *Love* is a way easier word to use out of the country.

"Do you want me to go talk to him for you?" she asked.

No, I was embarrassed. Also, I had a boyfriend. Sasha looked irritated. Since I had told her that I would by no means be marrying Trevor, she was ready for me to be done with it already. So I looked back at Aleg, who was still simmering.

Well . . . maybe he had a good idea for where we should go next? Maybe there was a wonderful local cultural event that he would know about. She could ask him about that, at the very least.

We got up and marched over to the beautiful bartender. Sasha started speaking to him in Russian, and they chatted for a couple of minutes while I did my Ulla routine, smiling and nodding whenever Aleg would look my way with those freakin' *eyes.*

After a couple of minutes, Sasha turned to me. "This is Aleg. I told him you like him. He likes you, too. You have a date with him tomorrow night. Don't say no, because you're not going to marry Trevor anyway, which means you're going to be single someday soon, which means it would be stupid to not go out with a Russian in Russia, which is the thing you're supposed to do in the place you're supposed to do it."

Sasha could make a great point.

I blushed, and Aleg reached out his hand. I put my hand in his, and he squeezed it.

"Priviet, Kristinichka." Hello, my little Kristin.

"How many years, how many winters."

Sweet Jesus.

Sasha called Aleg the next day, as promised, and chatted with him about where we would all meet. He asked to speak with me, and she handed me the phone.

"Priviet?" I tried.

"Hello, *Kristinichka,*" Aleg purred sweetly.

I giggled. "Hello, Aleg!"

A long beat, then he spoke again, sweetly, with so much hope: "Tonight?"

Aleg had learned an English word! I loved him. He was so smart.

"Dah! Tonight!" I trilled.

Another long beat, then:

"Kristinichka."

Another giggle, then, "Aleg."

Sweet Jesus.

Sasha and I hitched a ride to the bar where we would meet. As wildly dangerous as that sounds (and felt), that's how you got around Russia. There weren't enough taxis by a long shot, and so you just raised your hand, and then someone would pull over, ask you where you wanted to go, and tell you how much they would charge to take you there. Lots of people needed rides, and everyone who wasn't in the mob or the government (same people) needed extra money.

What this meant in practice was that two American girls would raise their hands. A beat-up car, usually containing one or two enormous, terrifying, glowering, mobster-looking men in black leather jackets, would pull over and ask, "Where to?" while swigging from a bottle of vodka. The American girls would decide whether the men were actually dangerous, or just dangerous-looking, like most Russians. (The Russian-born American girl was the first to note that, so it's more about self-loathing than xenophobia.)

We made a rule that we would only get in a car that contained fewer than two terrifying-looking giants, reasoning that we could overpower one three-hundred-pound Russian kidnapper, but two could get rapey. This all got less scary the more we did it, though, because inevitably the conversation with these gray-faced behemoths went something like this (in Russian):

SASHA: "Thanks for the ride. What's your name?"
GRAY-FACED BEHEMOTH: "Vlad. Where are you from?"
SASHA: "Los Angeles."
GRAY-FACED BEHEMOTH: "Hollywood! And you're

going to the Bolshoi tonight? Is [*insert famous dancer's name*] performing? He's remarkable. I saw him in *Swan Lake* and it made me weep. Also, you're going to love [*insert famous conductor's name*]. He squeezes emotion out of the orchestra like no one I've ever seen." [*Passing bottle of vodka over seat*] "Would you like a sip?"

Looks thus kept being deceiving, which made me very grateful to be with a Russian speaker. Because before Sasha would open her mouth, every single person in Russia looked at us as though they were going to kill us like they'd just killed their favorite dog when they realized they couldn't feed it through the winter.

"That's just what their faces look like," Sasha said to her mom one night.

Then she squeezed her mother's hand again.

On the night of my big date, we hitched a ride to the loud, dark club that Aleg had chosen for a meeting place. I had spent the day telling myself that meeting up with a guy did not mean I had to hook up with him—we were just making local friends!

Aleg showed up a few minutes after we ordered our *vodka tonica*s, and kissed me three times on the cheeks, right left right, the Russian way. What is important to understand about this custom is that you get one cheek kissed, then your noses and lips and eyes brush past each other's on your way to the other cheek, and then you do the whole pass and brush routine *yet another time* on your way back to the first cheek, breathing each other in the whole while. The slower the pass from one cheek to the next, the more serious the greeting. It's a pretty great way to spice up those hard, gray, vodka-and-snow-filled lives.

Aleg's passes were crazy slow.

Aleg immediately recognized a friend at the bar—Misha, a sexily dangerous-looking tattoo artist in his midthirties. Sasha immediately recognized that she needed to get a closer look at Misha's tattoo sleeves. So my translator left Aleg and me alone to get to know each other.

Aleg leaned over and screamed at me (it was very loud), "I speak small of English!"

"Fantastic!" I screamed back. "I'm kind of a talker, and the thought of what we were going to do if we couldn't communicate was sort of terrifying! So, are you from Moscow? How do you know Misha?"

Aleg looked at me, panicked for one beat, two, three . . . and then just kissed me.

He kissed the SHIT out of me. One thing that a tortured, dramatic worldview does for someone is it makes him a HELL of a kisser. At least, Sasha and I came to this understanding based on our sample size of two. Later in life I'd also find the same can be said about Israelis, who obviously share the Russian tortured, dramatic thing, combined with the whole "We may not even be here tomorrow and should try to make more Jews for the good of our people" Jewish thing. That particularly amps up the passion quotient. The tortured worldview kissing theory can even be true about regular Americans, if they're sensitive and unhappy enough.

So maybe my sample size is large enough. I'm sure my mother thinks so.

But back to the date. While Sasha could actually communicate with her new friend, it wasn't long before she, too, was gathering her own kissing data on the other end of the bar. The evening quickly turned into a veritable crazy-Russian-night-out stereotype: there was a lot of vodka, a lot of champagne, dirty dancing on a dance floor flooded with lots of flashing lights and fur-clad women shimmying to a combo of bad techno and bizarre American one-hit wonders that had apparently been huge in Russia. "Mambo No. 5" got a huge reaction, for example.

(A side note about Russian women: good God are they hot when they are eighteen. The girls in this club were all legs and cheekbones, pouty lips and exquisite big eyes. But, quite tragically, *every woman over forty* in Russia looks like a tiny, shriveled, ancient little gnome. That cold, pessimistic, vodka-and-cigarette-filled, fresh-vegetable-free life is *hard*—it drives over women's faces like a Soviet tank. Now that Sasha is a fantastic-looking forty, I can tell you it is not the genes, it is the life.)

Anyway, after some time dry humping to the Spin Doctors, Misha suggested we move the party back to his place, since Sasha was drunk enough to think that Misha was not too drunk to give her her very first tattoo.

We stumbled into a taxi with our bottles of vodka and champagne, and drove for a very, very long time. It turned out that Misha lived with his parents in a housing project on the outskirts of Moscow. Aleg did, too. Almost no one in Russia lives with fewer than two or three generations of family, and yet everyone has a dacha—a summer house. We were confused about how such impoverished people, who often had PhDs yet lived life ten to a room, could all afford summer homes, until we started noticing the small wooden shacks along the side of the highway. These were dachas. Apparently, when you've spent a Russian winter with ten relatives in one room, a week alone in a shack next to a highway equals an attractive option for your summer vacation.

We finally pulled up to Misha's towering tenement, and went up to the two-bedroom apartment, giggling and whispering as we snuck past his sleeping parents to Misha's room. But Misha's room was pretty small for four people trying to do terrible things to each other, and so Misha took Sasha for a twenty-minute tour of the bathroom, leaving me and Aleg to his futon.

Now, all day, when I wasn't thinking about how I absolutely was not going to cheat on my boyfriend, I had been harboring a very specific Aleg-related fantasy. It basically involved him teaching me how to say all of the parts of the body in Russian, by kissing each part and then telling me the word for it, which I would then repeat and try to remember as he moved to kiss the next spot. Then I would do the same for him, in English. It was really a very adorable fantasy.

So, after a day of this, I found myself on a futon with my Russian. And let's remember that I was twenty-eight, and had been with two people in the previous eight years. It had been a *very* long time since I had been with someone for the first time, and it hadn't happened very often. And Aleg and I could only communicate with our *eyes*, and our *bodies*. And we communicated *really effectively* that way. So everything was already fairly amazing when Aleg stopped doing something disgustingly wonderful, kissed the tip of my nose, and said:

"*Nos.*"

Nose. In Russian. HE WAS DOING IT! Delighted, I said "*nos,*" then kissed the tip of his nose and said "nose." Aleg repeated, a great student: "nose." Next was an ear. Fingers. Elbows. Terrible places.

Crazy, right?

Except it wasn't. I would eventually, via many other vacation romances, learn something: *This always happens when you make love to someone who speaks another language. Always.* It's crazy, but my fantasy apparently sprang from the fact that this is just a natural instinct for two people who cannot communicate and yet find themselves in the same room naked.

Sasha and Misha eventually returned, rumpled but smiling, for the second reckless portion of their evening together: the tattoo. My beautiful friend—fresh out of the Ivy League, the ultimate manifestation of the American Dream who had been saved from a life as just another angry-looking, prematurely aging Russian whose only way out of the country might have been as a mail-order bride—this young promising woman pulled down her pants, bent over a chair, and slurred at her new companion:

"Do whatever you want!"

Now, you might think that this should have been the moment where Sasha's good friend would intervene. But I was still topless, reasoning that as long as Aleg stayed on top of me, my modesty could remain intact. And so instead of intervening, I took another ladylike swig out of a bottle of champagne and slurred, "I love that you're doing this!"

"Are you gonna get one, too?" Sasha asked, as a very drunk Misha spilled his needles on the floor.

"Hell no!"

But Sasha still let Misha do whatever he wanted. Which turned out to be tattoing a large, misshapen (he was *so* drunk) infinity symbol made out of barbed wire on Sasha. It stretched across her entire lower back in a horizontal-ish figure eight-ish.

While Sasha got her tattoo, Aleg and I used her to get to know each other.

"Sasha, ask him where he was born."

"Sasha, how do you say, 'Your skin makes me cry?'"

In college, Sasha had invented a phrase that my friends and I all use to this day to describe that moment that happens when someone says something that you were completely sure only you had ever thought about. And which you then decide is a message from the universe that the two of you are supposed to be together forever. She called this thing a "moo-cow." The name came from a road trip she took with a college boyfriend. She was getting ready to break up with him, but on the trip driving through the country, the guy pointed at a passing cow and said, "Moo-cow." Now, that was what Sasha's family always said when they drove by cows, and so she took this moment as a sign that she was supposed to stay with the guy.

They broke up two months later.

Sasha always cautioned against the power of the moo-cow. Because a moo-cow feels *great*, but it can lead you down the wrong roads. It can make you stay with the wrong person, but, worse, it can make you break up with the *right* person just because the two of you never have any moo-cows, which, while they feel fantastic, are ultimately meaningless.

I was a *big* chaser of the moo-cow.

On that couch, through Sasha's translation, Aleg and I realized we had enough moo-cows to fill Red Square. And that, consequently, we were meant to find each other. First, we were born three weeks apart, in the same year. Crazy, right?! Second, we had both grown up during the Cold War, terrified that at any moment The Bomb would be dropped on us . . . by the other person's country! Furthermore, Aleg had been raised in a tiny town in far-eastern Russia, an eight-hour flight from Moscow, just across the sea from Japan. The only reason this town existed was that it contained a top-secret Russian military base . . . built around the nuclear missile launcher that his *father* was in charge of operating, and which was aimed at *Los Angeles . . . where I lived!* In terror of attack by the Russians! I was practicing my duck-and-cover *because of Aleg's father!* Who didn't want to drop a bomb on me any more than I wanted to drop one on his fucking hot son!

Now, again, this was just a few months after 9/11. The world was a scary, war-filled place. So it felt very natural to turn the sordid naked things I was doing in Russia while my boyfriend slept in our bed in Los Angeles into an act of international peacemaking. I was *literally* making love. Out of nothing at all. Love That Would Save Our Planet.

And that's how I used 9/11 to rationalize cheating.

But at least I didn't get a tattoo.

The next day, Aleg came with me in the taxi to the airport. We held each other tightly. I sang him "Leaving on a Jet Plane," and didn't feel embarrassed, like I absolutely should have. He knew some of the words.

"I don't know when I'll be back again. Oh, babe, I hate to go."

He held my face in his hands, and stared into my eyes with those *eyes*, and kissed me.

Moscow Sheremetyevo → Paris Charles de Gaulle
Departing: May 30, 2002

I flew from Moscow to Paris to meet my mom and stepdad and his kids for a couple of weeks of fighting in the South of France. I lit two candles in Notre Dame, one for Aleg and one for Trevor, feeling enough post-9/11 love swelling in my heart for both of them. While my angry family of five drove around Provence in a French car built for two, I channeled my new ability to sit quietly, and stared, peaceful, out the window at the fields of lavender and poppies as they argued.

Sasha changed her flight and stayed behind with Misha

for a couple of extra days. I would call her from pay phones in France, where she would chatter euphorically:

"I'm in Gorky Park eating hot dogs with Misha! Aleg misses you! We have to help them come to America! We'll help them get visas, Kristin! We'll CHANGE THEIR LIVES!"

She was not kidding, and I did not laugh. I just agreed, and cried, and told her to tell Aleg I missed him, too. Then I would call him, and, between a pay phone in France and a tenement on the outskirts of Moscow, we would coo the only words we could:

"Aleg?"

"Kristinichka."

"Aleg."

"Kristinichka."

Eventually, I paid a hundred and fifty dollars to leave my family in France twenty-four hours early, and Sasha paid the same to stay with Misha and leave Russia a few days late.

Back home, Sasha, somehow, through no fault of her own, turned out to be HIV-negative. As for me, I hid my travel journal and my pictures of Aleg in a box in Sasha's father's garage, and, racked with guilt, broke up with Trevor. And then, at twenty-nine, I went on what felt like my first adult date.

Before Russia, I thought I was fully cooked. I thought I was who I was going to be forever. But it turned out there was a little part of me that was still pink. That part was a little quieter, and less judgmental, and a lot wilder than the rest of me. Not quite Kristin ... more like Kristin-Adjacent. I'd spend the next ten years exploring this other part of myself that I found on a couch in a Russian tenement, and around dinner tables in Moscow. Even though it came at a morally inopportune moment, I had my first *Sex and the City* story. And that's how I became The Girl Who Never Lost Her Groove. The girl who was told by a depressive, hilarious friend, "You have more fun than anyone I know." The girl who got the most votes in a party game where everyone had to choose who they would switch lives with if they had to.

The Girl Who Was Terrified of Losing Her Groove.

3

"Two Ferris
Buellers Don't
Make
a Right"

Los Angeles International → *London Heathrow* →
Paris Charles de Gaulle
Departing: December 26, 2004

Have you ever fallen in love with someone you've never met? I have! And then I flew to Paris to go get him.

This next adventure requires a bit of context, so stay with me.

After my breakup with Trevor, I was determined to resist my natural instinct to fall into another long relationship. I went on more single-girl trips with Sasha, to China and Tibet, where the mountains, monks, and clay warriors were amazing and the men were too small and hairless, and to Spain, where I tussled with a Barcelonan who turned out to be wearing black panties that were identical to my own and who wanted to know if I liked things "a little bit strange." (He meant butt stuff. I do not.) I almost slipped back into relationshipland when I spent a New Year's Eve in the mountains of Canada making out with a good friend. For years he had been saying inappropriate drunken things about his hopes for us *if only we were both single.* He said I made him wonder what being with someone like me would feel like—meaning someone he could talk to, as opposed to his usual diet of inappropriately young waitresses. Then we finally were single, and kissed on a dance floor in Canada, but he promptly disappeared when we got back home, later explaining, "We really could have had something if you weren't so successful."

(Have I mentioned it can be a real bummer to be a working female writer in Los Angeles when it comes to dating? I don't want to use the words *boner killer* indiscriminately, but let's just say Sheryl Sandberg had some points about the likability of successful women. Also, not unrelated: Nell Scovell, the cowriter of *Lean In*, was a successful female sitcom writer.)

Anyway, I tried to be grateful that my friend's rejection kept me on track. My natural instinct was to search for love, but I was supposed to be enjoying my first taste of singledom, after all. So I continued running around Los Angeles declaring to anyone who asked that I was looking for a "great guy with commitment issues." And since pretty much all of the other women around me who were turning thirty were either getting married or getting panicked about not getting married, more than one guy in Los

Angeles liked the sound of that. If you are looking for the magic words that will make you into a Pied Piper to men, those are the ones. So I spent about a year leading rats around town with that particular flute, and then I met Ben.

Ben had something that turned out to be my own personal Pied Piper's trill: an epic, wildly flattering story of how we met. One that was so big and romantic that it *sounded* just like what I *thought* my How I Met Your Father story would sound.

The story went like this: one night, at a friend's birthday party, about a minute after I wondered if I was getting bored with my whole single-and-dating life, I re-met a girl who had apparently come to a Christmas party I had thrown almost a year earlier, just after my breakup with Trevor. When she put together that I was the girl who threw that party, she got very excited. Coincidentally, *just that week* she had had dinner with her old friend Ben, who was unhappily dating girls he wasn't liking. He complained that he couldn't stop comparing them to a girl he had briefly met at her Christmas party almost a year earlier ... ME! He had apparently been brought to my party by a mutual friend, and while I did not remember meeting Ben, he had been smitten. He hadn't had the courage to track me down and ask me out, but for a year he and his coworker at a production company would talk about the women Ben was dating, and he would always declare that they were "no Kristin Newman."

Who wouldn't like the sound of that?

Now, it's important to remember that this all happened in Los Angeles. And I looked like a thirty-year-old writer.

Not like a twenty-year-old model or actress or epically legged songstress, which is a category into which an alarmingly high percentage of Angelenas fall. And, because the city is so lousy with these leggy aliens, regular- to below-average-looking guys with reasonable employment levels *can actually get one*, another maddening aspect of being a woman in this city. So getting to be someone's standard-bearer in this dating pool was not something I expected.

Anyway, the story sounded like a story I would like to hear told for a lot of decades, especially at high school reunions, or in front of twenty-year-old actresses. So I let this girl set us up, and it turned out that Ben was a funny, smart, crazily intuitive guy with a dreamy voice. He came from a family of East Coast artists and writers who ran around Greenwich Village apartments and the family avocado ranch in California. (*Avocado ranch! With an ocean view!*) He could weave stories about the quirky characters in his family like a great novelist. Our e-mail repartee was like fireworks. He was a great kisser, and guitar player. And so, I thought, maybe a year of being single was enough. I thought this for a few months.

And then it started . . . *Why does he annoy me sometimes? Do I love him? Am I really ready for him to be The One? Shouldn't I feel more sure? I was sure with Vito. I wasn't sure with Trevor and I broke his heart. I don't want to break someone else's heart. He really likes me. Do I like him? Is it that I'm not ready yet? Why does he drive so slowly? Making a left turn should not make him this nervous.*

One day, a few months into our relationship, I decided I wasn't happy enough, and I broke up with Ben. We got back together a week later, because Ben's most special talent was an uncanny ability to see deep into my neurotic soul and talk me right off a cliff. During that get-back-together conversation, he also let me have it for being crazy, which I, upsettingly, discovered I found attractive. But during that week in between breaking up and getting back together, I went on a ski trip with two couples, and that's when I first heard about the man who led to this chapter's foreign adventure in Paris and London. A man I will call "Ferris Bueller."

It started with a simple postbreakup après-ski conversation in Mammoth over nachos and hot chocolates with one of my friends, a fellow TV writer:

"You know who you should meet, Kristin? This guy I work with—Ferris Bueller."

Immediately my friends' wives got big eyes and nodded resolutely—*yeah, do that*. They said the guy was a real-life Ferris Bueller, twenty years later. This was exciting because Ferris Bueller had been my Perfect Man since junior high—charismatic and fun, the guy who lit up the room, was loved by fancy bankers and school secretaries alike, and led great adventures with unfailing enthusiasm. I had crushed on another real-life Ferris throughout high school and college, but he had eventually become a professional lifeguard, which wasn't as appealing over thirty. So when I heard tell of a fully grown Ferris, with a successful career that didn't require a swimsuit at the office, I was excited.

My friends all said this Ferris was *just like me*—a

comedy writer with a big, enthusiastic personality who was always traveling, throwing great parties, and connecting people. He specialized in organizing trips to far-flung places and voraciously hunting movie-like life moments, just like I did. He even lived right around the block from me (which made the subsequent stalking much easier). But unlike me, he also came with mythical stories of the Ferris variety, often involving hundreds of people traveling around the world in costumes he dreamed up, skinny-dipping celebrities, and (his own) Andy Kaufman–esque public ass-shavings during fake wars with angry college lesbians. Oh, and one more thing:

He loved to do the thing you're supposed to do in the place you're supposed to do it.

Everyone was really sure Ferris and I would be the best setup anyone had ever seen. But, as almost everything does with a roomful of comedy writers, it soon turned into a bit. So as I struggled to carry my snowboard, one friend would pipe up, "Oh, Kristin, if Ferris were here he would *definitely* carry that for you." Then I would coo, "I know, he's so considerate."

In line for lunch: "Ferris is the best orderer. He'd definitely get you lunch if he were here." And I'd respond, "I know, his taste and manners are impeccable. I love him so much."

It soon progressed into an imaginary relationship: "You guys, do you think Ferris *loves me* loves me, or just *kinda* loves me?" "Oh, are you kidding?! He doesn't stop talking about you!"

By day two, the relationship started going through a rough patch: "Ferris just doesn't look at me the way he used to, guys." "No, Kristin, he does! He's over the moon! Everything's great!"

It was fun, and, in my party of five, with the two married couples and an empty spot next to me in bed where Ben was supposed to be, it legitimately cheered me up. The myth of "Kristin's Boyfriend, Ferris" took up so much conversational and mental space, it made me feel like I wasn't alone. I was there with *my boyfriend, Ferris.*

Which, of course, sounds insane.

But spending that much mental time with someone, whether they are there or not, apparently tells your brain something: *you love them.* I experienced the same weird phenomenon one time when I was trying to work up the courage to ask a platonic work friend to write a movie with me. He was very talented, and I was nervous he would say no because he didn't like the idea, or didn't think I was good enough to partner up with. So I spent the week kind of pining over him as a writing partner, and rehearsing how I would ask him to write with me. I would practice in my head, then chicken out, then mentally practice some more. Much like if you wanted to *ask someone on a date.* And that's when this weird thing happened: my practice conversations in my head started turning sexy. I would be imagining us writing, late at night, leaning over the same keyboard, faces close, when he would reach around me to type and . . .

Basically, the simple act of obsessing got the juices

flowing, and I created a temporary crush on my married colleague. And once I stopped obsessing about him as a writing partner, the crush disappeared, too.

Point being, apparently the brain can be tricked into love. So, even though I went home from the ski trip with my friends, and got back together with Ben a week later, a thought was stuck in my admittedly cuckoo head:

Are you sure you should get back together with Ben? Or should you give things a try with Ferris?

Which is when the interventions from Sasha and Hope started. "Ferris doesn't know you." "You don't know him." "This isn't real." "It's not Ferris versus Ben, because Ferris is imaginary." Nonsense like that.

Now, I'm not completely off my rocker, so I managed to put the whole business far enough back in my brain to get back together with Ben. And, a few months later, to finally say "I love you," and mean it. Of course that, too, was a bit of an ordeal. Because I had already broken up with him once, I made a list of rules I had to follow to make *sure* I meant it before I said the L word for the first time:

1. I couldn't say it while under the influence of alcohol.
2. I couldn't say it in any sort of hyperromantic situation, like on vacation or at a wedding.
3. I couldn't say it during sex.

The problem was, I only ever felt like saying it during one of the above scenarios. Watching Ben play the guitar in a condo on the lake in Tahoe after a joint and sex on a speedboat?! Signed, sealed, delivered! Sober, on a Tuesday at Baja Fresh? Not so sure. Which made me wonder if I meant it or not.

My friends also tried to intervene on these rules—when did I think most people felt like saying it for the first time? In line at the DMV? People generally say it drunk, having sex, in romantic locations. Which ultimately turned out to be true—the Three Big Words popped out of me one night when we went to a party thrown by a billionaire, got drunk, and snuck off to do it in the billionaire's child's tree house that was nicer than my actual house. I managed to break all three of my rules at once.

And the next day, I still loved him. But then we'd go to Baja Fresh the day after, and I'd wonder: *Did I?* And that's when I took all of that "love" and started making pro/con lists, which are both the death of love, and a good 10 percent of my journals. And, deep down, I kept wondering about Ferris.

Because every time I turned around, literally every month or two, someone else was coming up with the same great idea: *I know this guy who is the male version of you! You have to meet Ferris Bueller!*

They said that amazing things just happened when he was around, because he imagined them and then willed them into existence through personality alone. The stories about him were more epic with every telling. I had a boyfriend, but one I was torn about. And Ferris represented the possibility of being untorn, of being blissfully, 100 percent signed-sealed-delivered. And so I wondered.

So there I was, trying to forget about Ferris, the

summer that Sasha got married. It's hard to overstate how much Sasha getting married affected me. Aside from the fact that she was yet another friend going in a direction I was starting to fear I would never want to go, she was my partner in crime, my sister, my wild, funny, adventurous friend who helped teach me how to be wild and funny and adventurous.

And it wasn't just what was going on with Sasha's life that hit me in the face that weekend. Sasha's wedding weekend was one of those real-life moments that, if it were in a movie, would feel trite and convenient. She got married in New York, and also invited were Hope and our friend Ann, whose parents were a second family to me growing up. Ann had grown into a calm, organized lawyer who calmly married her college boyfriend and was now calmly nine months pregnant with the first baby any of our friends had produced. Hope was wildly depressed, and in the middle of an awful divorce from that boy she brought with us to Amsterdam, the one who snuck off to the sex show without her. And I was there with Ben . . . struggling with what I wanted to do next. We were a *Sex and the City* quartet: one marrying, one divorcing, one trying to decide if she's in love, one giving birth.

On the day of the wedding, Ann gave birth a few blocks away from the ceremony at precisely the moment Sasha said "I do," while Hope rolled her eyes at the promises of "forever," and I wept at losing my single buddy. Not those emotional, joyful, smiley wedding tears you shed because you're so happy. Big, heaving sobs of genuine grief sprang out of me as I stood under the chuppah, watching a person who felt like a piece of myself walk toward me, while somehow really walking away.

By the end of the weekend, I had lost my best girl. And when I got home, the old panic about Ben and my readiness to settle down continued. And so, after a tremendous amount of soul-searching, and self-created misery, and pro/con lists, I broke up with him again. Because . . . well . . . because. That's what I do. It sort of had something to do with the way he grocery-shopped. So . . . because of me.

I tortured myself *a lot*. I wept *a lot*. I doubted my decision *a lot*. I sat in my backyard crying to Sasha and her new husband, Jared.

"Why are you crying when *you* broke up with *him*?"

"Because I'm broken! He's great! And Trevor was great! I'm getting older, I should want to settle down! But I don't want to! Maybe I won't ever want to! Everyone else wants to, what's wrong with me? Maybe I'll sabotage all relationships forever because I'm broken!"

And they would assure me that I wasn't broken. That Trevor and I just weren't a match. Sasha's husband wrote me an actual guarantee on which he staked *ten thousand dollars* that I would meet a man I wanted to marry within the next five years.

"*Five years?!*" I wailed.

"You said you weren't ready yet."

"But I should be ready in sooner than *five years!*"

"I'm sure it will be sooner. I just want to make sure I don't lose the bet," he replied.

A few years ago, I found the guarantee, and saw that

Jared's marriage-guarantee date had passed years before, and cried again. He owes me ten thousand dollars to this day.

So it was while in this place that, out of the blue, I finally met Ferris. He just walked into a restaurant and sat down at my table.

I was at a big group dinner, and, without my knowledge, he had also been invited. (Coincidence! Fate!) He was late, and so I was nibbling on a salad when this friendly, boisterous guy walked in and shouted, "Hello!!!!" The guy had an entirely shaved head, save for two small, round patches of three-inch-long black hair that were sprouting out of the top, a little off-center, apparently the result of a bet. He certainly stood out, but not in a hot way. Just in a jolly and poorly coiffed way. The stranger sat down, and offered me his hand:

"Hi! I'm Ferris Bueller."

And there he was.

While fireworks did not exactly go off, it really didn't matter. I had already decided the truth based on "Ferris Bueller: The Myth": we were meant for each other. And The Real Ferris Bueller was certainly cute enough aside from the hair polka dots on his skull, and likable as hell. But that didn't really matter.

Because after all these months, and all these people telling me he was perfect for me, I had fallen in love with him. Like, really in love, in a way that made my friends hold interventions since I *had never met him*. Like, in love like

I've written TV shows for major networks with characters based on him. More than one. In love like I eventually flew to Europe to try to kiss him.

And, finally, here is that story:

A couple of months into my Ferris-stalking fever, Ferris organized the first of what would be yearly New Year's Eve trips that I spent the next decade going on. The trips usually consist of twenty to sixty people going wherever in the world Ferris tells them, and having the most ridiculous, high-profile, memoir-worthy adventures imaginable. There was even an article about Ferris's usually costume-bedecked excursions in the *New York Times*. He's taken us to chalets in the Alps, jillionaires' estates in Punta del Este, beach houses in the Dominican Republic, twenties masquerade balls in San Francisco, Brazil, Portugal, the Bahamas. Last month, he and his merrymaking right-hand man Thomas sent out an e-mail to hundreds of people, telling them to show up on a Thursday night with a passport and three hundred dollars for a mystery three-day international adventure. Sixty people ended up on a bus to Mexico.

This first trip was to Paris, where Ferris's brother was an Episcopal minister at the American Cathedral, which is located just off the Champs-Élysées. Ferris was throwing a party *in the cathedral* on New Year's Eve. And while I was not "invited" per se, the friends who had first suggested I date Ferris on that weekend in Mammoth were, and promised it was a "come one come all" sort of affair. So the next time I ran into Ferris, I informed him that I was going to be in London, by coincidence, and he said of course I should come to the party in Paris, and then I grabbed my cousin Emma, and she grabbed her awful friend Sally, and we bought tickets to London and Paris.

A little on my travel partners: my cousin Emma is two years older than I am. Growing up, she had an amazing Dorothy Hamill haircut and I wanted to be just like her. She married her first college sweetheart at twenty-five, when I was living with my first college sweetheart, Vito, in Vail, working three ski-town jobs to afford my six months as a "ski bum."

It was these similar starts—long-term relationships with guys we both met at eighteen and both thought we would be with forever—that made what happened with Emma so resonant for me. Basically, while I had a wrenching breakup after six years with my guy, she married hers (thereby breaking my "don't choose your spouse young" rule). But after thirteen years, she found that he had become just a best friend. So they officially separated.

She got back out there, single and living alone for the first time at thirty-two, and met men who woke up something in her that she had never even realized existed. And she found me again. Just as I was breaking up with Trevor, single at thirty for what felt like the first time in my adult life.

Emma finally filed her divorce papers just before we left for Paris. Like me, she had few friends left who were still single, and so eagerly jumped on a trip that would be filled with dozens of new single strangers. I knew Emma would mix easily with this new posse, because she's the most easygoing person in the world, up for anything, capable, and cheerful. Her friend Sally was not.

Before I launch into what was wrong with Sally, I think I should share a few thoughts on what makes one a good traveler. I probably should say that this is what makes you a good traveler *in my opinion*, but deep down I really think this is just universal, incontrovertible truth. There is the right way to travel, and the wrong way. And if there is one philanthropic deed that can come from this book, maybe it will be that I teach a few more people how to do it right. So, in short, my list of what makes a good traveler, which I recommend you use when interviewing your next potential trip partner:

1. You are open. You say yes to whatever comes your way, whether it's shots of a putrid-smelling yak-butter tea or an offer for an Albanian toe-licking. (How else are you going to get the volcano dust off?) You say yes because it is the only way to really experience another place, and let it change you. Which, in my opinion, is the mark of a great trip.

2. You venture to the places where the tourists aren't, in addition to hitting the "must-sees." If you are exclusively visiting places where bus-loads of Chinese are following a woman with a flag and a bullhorn, you're not doing it.

3. You are easygoing about sleeping/eating/comfort issues. You don't change rooms three times,

you'll take an overnight bus if you must, you can go without meat in India and without vegan soy gluten-free tempeh butter in Bolivia, and you can shut the hell up about it.

4. You are aware of your travel companions, and of not being contrary to their desires/needs/schedules more often than necessary. If you find that you want to do things differently than your companions, you happily tell them to go on without you in a way that does not sound like you're saying, "This is a test."

5. You can figure it out. How to read a map, how to order when you can't read the menu, how to find a bathroom, or a train, or a castle.

6. You know what the trip is going to cost, and can afford it. If you can't afford the trip, you don't go. Conversely, if your travel companions can't afford what you can afford, you are willing to slum it in the name of camaraderie. P.S.: Attractive single people almost exclusively stay at dumps. If you're looking for them, don't go posh.

7. You are aware of cultural differences, and go out of your way to blend. You *don't* wear booty shorts to the Western Wall on Shabbat. You *do* hike your bathing suit up your booty on the beach in Brazil. Basically, just be aware to show the culturally correct amount of booty.

8. You behave yourself when dealing with local hotel clerks/train operators/tour guides etc. Whether it's for selfish gain, helping the repu-

tation of Americans traveling abroad, or simply the spreading of good vibes, you will make nice even when faced with cultural frustrations and repeated smug "not possible"s. This was an especially important trait for an American traveling during the George W. years, when the world collectively thought we were all either mentally disabled or bent on world destruction. (One anecdote from that dark time: in Greece, I came back to my table at a café to find that Emma had let a nearby [handsome] Greek stranger pick my camera up off our table. He had then stuck it down the front of his pants for a photo. After he snapped it, he handed the camera back to me and said, "Show *that* to George Bush." Which was obviously extra funny because of the word *bush*.)

9. This last rule is the most important to me: you are able to go with the flow in a spontaneous, non-uptight way if you stumble into something amazing that will bump some plan off the day's schedule. So you missed the freakin' waterfall— you got invited to a Bahamian family's post-Christening barbecue where you danced with three generations of locals in a backyard under flower-strewn balconies. You won. Shut the hell up about the waterfall.

Sally did not adhere to any rule from the above list. She never ate or slept or moved when Emma and I did. She was not constitutionally capable of noticing what anyone around her wanted or needed. She fought with every person with whom she came in contact, in hotels and train stations, in cabs and museums. We spent the entire two-week trip apologizing for her.

But we had high hopes when we landed in London, where we would pass a few days warming up for New Year's Eve in Paris. We spent those days primarily just trying to get Sally out of bed. She had awful jetlag, but insisted on going without the sleeping aids Emma and I popped until she had tossed and turned for several hours . . . which meant that she was taking an eight-hour sleeping pill just before Emma and I were waking up. After giving her a couple of hours while we got dressed and ate breakfast, we would try to quietly leave her to sleep. But she would wake up and insist on coming with us just as we were ready to slip out the door. So we would take off our coats and get comfortable while Sally ran a nice long bath, and our days would get started in the early afternoon.

One night, a couple of hours after Sally woke up, we went out to dinner in Soho to a Thai restaurant that sat parties at communal tables. We were seated with a group of six people from Mauritius, which, it turns out, is an island nation in the Indian Ocean, about twelve hundred miles east of Africa. The country is a mix of Indian, African, and French descendants, and if this little table of gorgeously colored people was any indication, the mix is a good one. They were all twenty- and thirtysomething, and most of them were "barristers" in London. Isn't it funny how when people tell you they're a "lawyer" it's super boring, but when they tell you they're a "barrister" it feels like you're meeting Colin Firth? As John Travolta said, "It's the little differences."

One of the female barristers was there with her younger brother, a pretty, twenty-year-old, effete fashion-industry type who was living in New York City. We all made friends over dinner, and I made eyes with one particularly handsome, dark-eyed twenty-four-year-old named Nicolas, who said he wanted his picture taken kissing my cheek. I thought that was a great idea. After dinner, he invited us to come dancing with them.

Nicolas suggested a club nearby that he said had a fantastic DJ, and which he said was mixed—both gay and straight. That sounded perfect since we were so clearly a mixed group—or, at least, a group of straight people with the one obviously gay young brother from New York. So our new posse of nine spilled down the wet streets arm in arm and piled into the club, which was filled with rainbow disco lights; mirrored floors, ceilings, and walls; and exclusively tan, waxed, shirtless men whose thongs were showing above their white jeans. This club was as "mixed" as the Village People. But the DJ was indeed fantastic, and so I grabbed my barrister and hit the dance floor.

The nice thing about a gay club is there is no possible way to be the sluttiest person in the room. Nicolas was a hell of a dancer, and our bodies were moving really well, and really close. It didn't take long for some kissing and groping to spring out of this fertile soil. He tasted like orange-vanilla lollipop, and it was all pretty sexy. If there is one thing that is my favorite thing in the world, it's making out on a dance floor. Of course, it's not always the most ladylike thing to be caught doing. I have more pictures from college than I'd like of me, twenty pounds heavier, in some nice Midwestern boy's arms, looking caught and squinty-eyed, lipstick smeared across my round, stuffed-pizza-stuffed cheeks, maybe a nipple or two accidentally poking out over the strapless dress I'd borrowed from my thinner roommate . . . So, not the classiest. But here in this gay club in London, squeezed in between about a thousand men with their hands on each other's Disneylands (happiest places on earth), I could quietly hump this stranger's leg and still come across like one of the daughters from *Downton Abbey*.

I found more evidence of my relative sense of decorum when I went to the bathroom, and had to squirm my way through the sea of humping men. It reminded me of when I was a kid and we would go play in the waves at night when the grunion were running. We'd scream as we ran across the sand covered with millions of slimy, squirming, mating fish, slithering all over each other and our toes . . . Crossing this dance floor was like that, but with more boners and bronzer.

Anyway, I made it to the women's bathroom to find that the door had two signs on it: one that read WOMEN, and a second that clarified WOMEN ONLY ALLOWED IN WOMEN'S RESTROOM!!! *NO MEN!!!* Once I pushed that door open, which was difficult due to the fact that the room was filled wall to wall with men, I found two stalls with signs of their own on the doors: ONE PERSON AT A TIME IN STALL!!! Each stall had two to four sets of male feet inside.

I managed to beg my way to a moment with a toilet,

and peed amongst the smell of cocaine and sounds of coupling/throupling, then made my way back to Emma and Sally, who sat with our Mauritian friends. Nicolas and Raj, the young gay New Yorker, talked to two older white-haired-and-jeaned gentlemen nearby, while Raj's older sister, Leoni, watched in amusement.

"Poor Raj," she said. "These guys won't leave him alone. And that one could be his father."

Raj was whispering into the older man's ear, and smiling. Whatever he was saying was making the old man smile, too.

One of the Mauritians leaned over to Raj's sister: "Leoni, I don't think he minds."

Leoni looked confused, and turned back to watch her brother, an idea slowly dawning. And that's when we understood that not only did she not know her brother was gay, which was sort of like not noticing he had two arms and two legs, but the entire reason we were here tonight was so that her friends could help him come out via the fascinating approach of making out with old men in front of his sister. We had stumbled into a Mauritian coming-out party.

Leoni started rocking back and forth, trying to self-soothe by saying things like, "I'm in the ocean surrounded by dolphins, I'm in the ocean surrounded by dolphins," as she threw back her margarita and watched her brother grind on the hot, tan grandpa.

We whispered among ourselves how incredible it was that she hadn't seen that this obviously gay boy was gay as he and my date got pawed by the silver-haired men. I got up to grab Nicolas, who had been ignoring me completely while he was wing-manning for his friend . . . really well. *Like, he didn't seem to mind it at all, actually.* And then I realized that I, too, was not noticing that someone had two arms and two legs.

I slept next to Emma that night.

Sally, though, brought home a barrister. They got a second room for the two hours we had before we needed to wake up to catch our train to Paris, and Sally stumbled into our room to pack one hour and fifty minutes later. Realizing she had lost an earring in the other, now vacated, room, she called the front desk demanding to be let back in. But the room was under the barrister's name, who had already left.

"You guys, what was that guy's name?" she called to us irritably, still on the phone with the front desk.

We, too, did not know the name of the man with whom she had just had sex, so she yelled at the front desk for a few more minutes. "So I don't know his name! You saw me come in two hours ago with that guy, you know I was with him in his room, just let me in!" She was clearly much more attached to this earring than she was to her dignity.

Now, let's not get distracted by my sexy night with the gay Mauritian. I was in Europe because I invited myself on a trip across oceans so that I could have a wildly romantic New Year's with the man of my dreams. The man who, even if we hadn't fallen in love *yet*, after months of knowing each other, was still ensconced in my little head as my best

hope for finding someone who would make me want wh
everyone else in the world seemed to want. This is a lot
of pressure. And that pressure built up mostly about two
inches below my left eye, on my cheekbone, in the form of
an enormous, painful, tumorlike pimple. The kind of pimple that even Emma and Sally had to admit was the kind
that makes you skip prom, the kind that stars in a Stridex
commercial.

Our first night out in Paris, I carefully put spackle on
my face, trying my best to look less like an awkward teenager, and we went to our first Ferris-organized dinner.

I've now shared a hundred group dinners with Ferris,
and they always go the same way. He introduces everyone,
making every member of the party sound like the most
incredible person in the world. He does all of the order-
ing while everyone gabs. He's a perfect orderer. The tables
are boisterous, people feed one another from communal
plates, there are often performances of the singing or trick-
performing or toast-making variety, attractive strangers at
adjacent tables are usually brought over to join the party,
and the waiters or chefs or restaurant owners often end up
sitting with us, sharing a bottle of wine and handing over
their phone number to Ferris so he'll invite them to his
next party. It's magical. And as the person who normally
takes responsibility for the success of any given dinner
party, I am always both impressed and vaguely displaced.

Ferris is better at what I'm great at.

So we walked into the private room that held this first
dinner, excited to see what Ferris had cooked up. It turned
out that Ferris had flown to Paris from Berlin, where he

ul blond stranger in the terminal. She
he next Bond girl, and had a part in the
She was that kind of blond girl. On the
iness class and she was in coach, and
champagne and warm nuts back to her during
the flight and discovered she would be staying with some
model friends just a couple of blocks from his brother's cathedral! So lucky! So she and some Latvian models were
now part of our party. And were the center of attention. I
didn't need to worry about my pimple being noticed . . . or
any of the rest of me.

"God bless how many beautiful women Ferris always
rounds up," one male guest said to me, not implying I was
one of them.

Now, despite my focus on Ferris, it was also impossible
not to notice how many other attractive, funny, single men
were in this group. The seeds of many crushes I would
have over the next few years were planted on this trip. But
what I didn't understand yet was that few of these guys
were available to me, really.

They were all Peter Pans, and, as I had yet to accept
that I was a Pietra Pan myself, I didn't see it. Over the
years, more than one of them would eventually give me
some speech that added up to the notion that I was "not
one to be trifled with." That you didn't kiss someone like
me if you didn't want to marry her, and that was far, far
too scary a proposition. This "compliment" frustrated me
many a night, in the face of chemistry with one friend or
another who just wouldn't kiss me.

But somehow I didn't learn all of this at that first dinner . . . despite it being under my nose, right next to my pimple.

We did ultimately have a great night. We went out dancing, and I met all of these amazing, hilarious women who were also part of the trip, and danced with the charming men. Where most of my friends at home had fallen into the "married" or "bitter to be single" categories, here was a group of thirtysomething single people who were *delighted* to be single in their thirties. Their careers were starting to take off, and the combination of the newfound money no one had had in their twenties and the freedom they all protected like mama bears with their cubs was a heady brew. I would learn that this group entering a bar is a thing of beauty: within moments, everyone will split up and immediately make new friends in every corner, and they will all, ultimately, be dancing in one another's collective arms by the end of the night. We owned every room we entered. I was pining for Ferris, but I was also having the best time of my life.

New Year's Eve arrived. Now, while I was not exactly "connecting" with Ferris, and was starting to wonder if perhaps he and I were perhaps a little *too* alike, he had not yet hooked up with any of the models or Bond girls he had collected. And so I was still holding out hope for a midnight kiss moment, involving fireworks and chilly Parisian night air, that would deliver on everything the trip (and the rest of my life) was supposed to be.

Emma, Sally, and I made our way through wintery

Paris to Ferris's party at the American Cathedral. Ferris's brother's stone-and-stained-glass priest's apartment in the church was filled with food and music and people in gorgeous dresses and tuxedos, velvet smoking jackets and feather boas, Givenchy gowns and seventies ruffled thrift-store shirts. There were what turned out to be members of the Parisian Algerian mafia, who had given their number to Ferris "in case shit went down." (Shit never went down, but that number got a lot of cool tables at impossible-to-get-into Parisian clubs.) There were guys who managed the finances of sovereign nations and *New Yorker* cartoonists and a Brit in "public relations" who would spend the next eight years in Iraq and Afghanistan as one of General Petraeus's closest advisors. Ferris had met dozens of Parisians during his month in town, and they mixed with his other guests, who had flown in from all over the U.S. and Europe. It had only taken Ferris a couple of weeks to become a hub in Paris, just like he was at home.

A wrought-iron spiral staircase stood in the middle of the living room, and it disappeared into what turned out to be the cathedral's bell tower, which looked out over the Eiffel Tower, and all of Paris. Over the course of the evening, people would bundle up and carefully climb the stairs in stilettos, up up up through three stories of the windy, pigeon-filled stone tower, trying not to fall through the grates or spill their champagne.

Ferris was wearing a blue velvet tux that he has worn every New Year's since. (I just texted him to confirm that he never washes the tux. He responded: "The yearly Halloween cow costume never gets washed, but should. The blue velvet tux doesn't really need cleaning." So . . . no. He never washes it.) Anyway, back on that first magical night when the tux was still clean, Ferris came over to welcome us with two bottles: one a three-foot-tall double magnum of red wine, and the other a bottle of absinthe he had smuggled in from Berlin. He poured us glasses of both, happily spilling red wine that could not possibly be successfully poured from so large a bottle. He looked ecstatic that I was there, and kissed me on both cheeks, European-style, and gushed about how beautiful I looked . . . and then did the same to everyone else.

That was about how the night went. I circled Ferris, he circled away. Another friend gave me a quick awkward peck at midnight, at the top of the bell tower, while we all huddled together on the freezing, tiny balcony and watched the fireworks I had imagined going off over my midnight kiss instead going off over all of Paris.

But the party raged on. Thomas, Ferris's right-hand man and fellow magic-maker, did a late-night striptease from his tuxedo down to a gold Speedo that I have now seen on New Year's Eves all over the world. This first striptease happened on the spiral staircase just as the church deacon entered the room. A couple of guys chased me around unsuccessfully as I unsuccessfully chased Ferris. (I call this phenomenon a *Pirates of the Caribbean* night, after the part in the ride where a fat woman chases a man who chases a pretty woman, all in a circle, no one ever catching anyone.)

The night finally ended at six in the morning, because Ferris's brother had to give a sermon at nine. I stumbled out of the cathedral with my sixty new friends, happy and disappointed in equal measure. I hugged Ferris good-bye and clip-clopped home.

The next "morning," I woke up at about one p.m., left Emma and Sally behind to sleep, and took myself out to breakfast for my first moment alone. I found a perfect little warm café, and the sun came out for the first time on the trip, and it reflected off the rain-soaked Église Sainte-Marie-Madeleine across the way and straight onto my face, almost blinding in its intensity and warmth. La Madeleine is a neoclassical cathedral completed in 1842 that looks like an ancient Greek temple. It's beautiful, but, in my opinion, it's trying to be something it isn't. I teared up—at the bigness of my hopes that had been dashed, and the incredible group of open, warm, hilarious, attractive, happy weirdos I had managed to find, at my luck that I was eating madeleines while I stared at the Madeleine in Paris on the first day of the year, at the sun that shone on my healing pimple. After breakfast, I walked into the cathedral, and got down on my knees, and gave thanks. I hadn't found true love, but I had stumbled onto the people who were going to make my life without it happier. My life was starting to become what it was supposed to be.

I would eventually realize that I didn't want to be with Ferris any more than he wanted to be with me—we were way too much alike. Remember that in the movie, Ferris doesn't date a female Ferris. He dates Sloane—the one on the ground looking up at him adoringly as he goes by on the float, wondering, *How does he do it?* I wasn't that girl. I wanted to be up on the float.

When Ferris came home from Paris, he invited a big group of friends over for food and reminiscing. And I was one of the people he invited. I walked into the house that I had walked by so many times when I was stalking Ferris the stranger, and a dozen people threw their arms around me. By not making out with any of the men in the group, I was embraced by the girls, who distanced themselves from the many fluttering women this posse of attractive, successful, single guys always attracted. Being part of this world of people who were *happily* single in their thirties, who knew how to live life in a brave, big way, felt better than humping the leg of a gay barrister.

Ben tried to get back together again, and as tempted as I would be by the completeness of his love in the face of a new world of men who seemed to see me as some sort of little brother, something deep within me was screaming that I wasn't ready to be half of a whole. I was about to be having too much fun.

4

"Love the Juan You're With" (Argentina, Part 1)

Los Angeles International → *Buenos Aires Ezeiza*
Departing: March 15, 2005

In really important ways, Argentina was my first love. It was the first place I went all by myself, and I fell in love with it hard. A little because of how Argentina made me feel about me, in the way you fall in love with that crush at summer camp because he's the first person who's ever looked at you *like that*. Argentina made me feel backlit, like the girl who makes the music swell when the camera hits her, like the girl who first broke your heart.

I ended up in Argentina because my friends seemed to think that having imaginary boyfriends who didn't like me back was a sign I needed something . . . different. And so they secretly signed me up for Internet dating, "winking" and messaging men as me before finally showing me their top choices. I had never Internet dated, mostly because I wanted a better, more star-crossed how-we-met story than that. Sasha and Hope decided that was stupid, and that I needed someone like them to take charge of my romantic life. They found me a supposedly straight guy who drove a Volkswagen Bug. Not a cool vintage one, a new one. With a bud vase.

Depressing, right?

I had one season left of my seven-year run on *That '70s Show*, which meant it was my last spring hiatus to spend traveling—the next year I would have to stick around more to find a new job. But everyone with whom I normally traveled was either overemployed or underemployed or too married or too pregnant to travel. And so there was . . . a VOID.

"Kristin, a void is a *good* thing," my mother said. "You're always rushing to fill up your life with fun fun fun. But nothing new or good can come in without a void to fill. Voids are *necessary* and *wonderful.*"

So I spent about a week after my work year ended just *being* in all of that voidy space, just feeling all of that sweet *nothing* . . . and then I bought a one-way ticket to Argentina.

My mother really shouldn't have been surprised, about either my ambivalence regarding settling down, or my desire to travel south. I was at least third generation in both departments. My mother loved Latin America, and as I mentioned before, part of the reason she and my father divorced after eighteen years was because she wanted to live a bigger, sexier, more international life. So they split up, and when I was fifteen and she was thirty-eight, she and I both started dating for the first time.

"Who the hell is going to go out with her?" Sasha and I wondered about my petite, pretty, charismatic, and successful mother, who when she wasn't working hundred-hour weeks was skiing, scuba diving, and preparing gourmet meals. "I hope she's not jealous when I start having lots of dates and she doesn't," I added, dipping another Oreo into peanut butter and shoving it into my pudgy, acne-covered face. "Kill me if I'm trying to find a guy in my thirties."

She did okay. Like *Sex and the City* okay. She even had cute, objectifying nicknames for the men she met: there was Donut Man (he introduced himself by buying her a donut), Cape Man (he came to their first and only date unironically wearing a cape), Nervous Breakdown in the Caracas Airport Man (self-explanatory). The man she finally fell in love with was a dashing European-born, American-educated businessman who lived in Mexico City . . . and who broke her heart. His name was Laszlo, but Sasha gave him a cute nickname: "Promiser of Everything and Deliverer of Nothing."

Laszlo wouldn't move to the States, and my mom wouldn't leave me and my grandma to move to Mexico, and so she lost him to a twentysomething aerobics instructor who lived down his street. But her love of Latin America preceded and survived the breakup, and that came from *her* mother.

My mother's mother left the family farm in Iowa for California when she was seventeen, and never saw her own mother again. She met my grandfather at work at an aerospace company, but he would only marry her if she quit working and stayed home with the kids. Because my grandmother was born when she was (and because she also happened to be pregnant with my mother), she quit, had my mother and her two siblings, and reported waking up in the morning to their little voices, thinking, *Oh, God, I have to get through another day*. My mom would describe cleaning days in her house as a child, when my grandmother would go into "rages" about being a housewife. She wrote haikus in her head as she ironed to keep herself from "losing her mind."

The minute my grandmother's three kids were out of the house, my old white grandma went back to school at Compton Junior College (as in *Straight Outta Compton*), and signed up for a foreign exchange program in Mexico. She left my grandfather behind for a couple of months, and some Mexican family who signed up for an American college student got my grandmother. I still feel sorry for that seventeen-year-old Mexican boy who must have had so many fantasies about showing around his wide-eyed, nubile American "sister."

So the women on one side of my family were travelers. But my paternal line was just the opposite. Just as my mother loved to roam and my father loved to watch the sun set over his own backyard, their parents were similarly split. My dad's father had only been out of the country for his military tour in World War II, which he always called "a wonderful adventure," but never repeated. (He would show me pictures that he had taken from the deck of his naval ship of bombs blowing up gorgeous South Pacific beaches, and simply comment, "Look at that beautiful beach.")

My dad's mother traveled even less. She had French ancestors, and so embraced France in all of the ways one can embrace France if one is limiting one's embrace of France to hanging paintings of France around one's house. She exclusively decorated with what she called "my Frenchie colors," and collectible plates of French street scenes that she bought in the gift section of the Cracker Barrel. Finally, when they were grown, her kids started a "Send Mom to Paris" fund, which they would all add to on Christmas and her birthday. But she cut it off after only a couple of contributions. She didn't want to go to Paris.

I asked her about that once, not long before she died. Why wouldn't she want to go to the place that was her "favorite place"?

"I was afraid it wouldn't live up to my dreams," she said.

So it was my maternal line's wandering, ambivalent soul that made its way to me. And at thirty-one, I had one regret in my life: I had never lived in another country. I decided to dodge depression and the dates my friends were finding me on the Internet by spending this last job-hunt-free hiatus *pretending* that I lived in another country for a few months.

I knew no one in Buenos Aires, and I was a little terrified. I would say the terror was evenly split between fear for my safety and fear of disappointment. But I didn't want to be my grandmother, never going to Paris in case it was a letdown, so I took a deep breath and went.

I had the numbers of a few friends of friends who lived in town. I got an apartment in Palermo, a lovely neighborhood near the Central Park of Buenos Aires, and an Argentine cell phone, and signed up for daily Spanish and tango classes. I called every friend of a friend within twenty-four hours of landing in Argentina, and had dinner plans my second night there.

Fuck you, Void!

Within a week I had met a group of expats from the U.S. and England and Malaysia, and had my first date with a *porteño* (resident of Buenos Aires). It was with a man I met at La Viruta, a *milonga*, or tango club, which was located in the basement of an Armenian community center. Victor was either a construction worker, or an architect. (I'd had only a week of Spanish classes at that point.) Before our first date, I asked Kate, a quiet, awkward American girl who had lived in Argentina for five years, what it was like to date Argentinos.

"Well, they expect you to sleep with them on the first date, because that's what Argentine women do," she told me.

"Huh. And what do they do when you don't?" I asked.

Kate shrugged shyly, legitimately stumped. "I don't know."

I met my Argentine lover at a party on the outskirts of Buenos Aires, in a country club that was promoting the opening of its new golf course. The local girls who brought me said that the event was very "*fashion*," their highest compliment. The crowd was a mix of models, actors, and *porteño* elite, who all mixed in the warm night.

Mechi, the *fashion* party girl who brought me, told me she wanted me to meet someone. That someone would become the most important vacation romance of my life. Father Juan.

Father Juan is not a priest, sadly, but he had just recently left a Catholic seminary where he had spent four years studying to become one, so that's what I secretly called him. To his face I eventually started calling him "*Dulce*," short for *dulce de leche*, because his skin is the color and smoothness and sweetness of a baby covered in Argentine caramel.

Father Juan has the combination of ethereal and sexy beauty that melts hearts of single American girls and praying congregations alike. Juan as an actual priest would have turned very *Thornbirds* very fast. Evidence: his nickname for me was "*Pulpa*"—a feminized form of the Spanish word for *octopus*. Because when he tried to get out of bed, I would wrap my tentacles around him, not letting him go.

I learned later that it was very rare for someone from Juan's socioeconomic class to become a priest. He grew up in English schools, in the fanciest neighborhood in Buenos Aires, with country weekend houses and an apartment in New York and a beach house in Punta del Este and a family Arabian-horse ranch in the pampas. But at twenty-six, he decided to become a Catholic priest, and spent four years eating, basically, gruel, in the service of Our Lord Jesus Christ.

And away from women.

That night, though, he was just a guy at a party. Mechi introduced us, and Juan said hello, quietly and respectfully. And, despite the fact that I am not convinced that Jesus was anything other than a world-changing ethicist, I thanked Jesus.

Juan has a sort of internal light that just radiates out of him, the kind of light you would think a man of the cloth *should* have, because it makes you believe in God. Yes, he's six feet tall, with broad shoulders, flawless golden-brown skin, silky black hair, and this big, white, leading-man smile. But the first thing you really notice about Father Juan is just this beaming *sweetness*. It's fairly devastating.

His friends danced and drank and chased models while Juan and I chatted about horses. He loved horses the way a child loves horses. He loved a lot of things like a child. Years later, I found a CD of children's music in his collection . . . that he bought for himself. There was just a simplicity and sincerity and utter lack of edge to him that probably would have gotten boring . . . eventually. I imagine. It's hard to say, because he was just so ridiculously beautiful and sweet that everything he said and did was fascinating.

He was shy, and I wasn't sure if he liked me. But soon

we were slow-dancing, and at the end of the night he asked me if I wanted a ride home.

In the front seat of his little red car, Juan kissed me. The kiss was just like him, sweet and sexy at the same time. And then he drove me home, and asked if he could come up, and I of course said he could, and then he did something that no Latin lover has ever done in the history of Latin lovers . . .

He didn't have sex with me.

We did naked stuff, don't get me wrong. There was no chance I wasn't going to put my lips on as much of that beautiful skin as was humanly possible. But The Deed was never on the table. After a few hours, Juan got up to go, and I felt in the darkness for my camera. When you reach the top of Everest, you want evidence. I couldn't see him dressing in the dark, so I just pointed the camera in his general direction, and started shooting.

FLASH. Juan's smooth perfect back, as he gets out of bed.

FLASH. Juan, pulling a shirt over his head, his perfect flat brown belly exposed.

FLASH. Juan, laughing, covering his face with his hand.

FLASH. Juan back on the pillow, smiling as I kiss his ear.

Juan and I spent the next two months dating casually. By which I mean that I obsessed about him constantly, and he casually dated me. I met a couple of his friends, I saw him a couple of times a week. The Deed continued to be a non-starter, but Juan taught me words like *mimitos*, which are little snuggles and caresses. And *mimitos* with Father Juan felt like they could knock a girl up.

But he kept me at arm's length. I think I was a lot for him, this sweet, slow-moving guy who had just left the seminary, and was now back in college. (He was getting his degree in marketing. I met another guy once who had left the Episcopalian monkhood, and he went back for his degree in marketing, too. I guess spreading the Good News is essentially a sales job.)

To keep myself from staring at my four photos of Father Juan all day, I went to my Spanish class with the other foreigners, and I studied tango with my tiny dance teacher who wouldn't let me do anything but walk in a circle for a week, à la *The Karate Kid*. I went out to dinner at midnight and went dancing at two in the morning, and, like a real *porteña*, never ever slept.

And I met a lot of other Juans.

So many Juans that it led to cheap Juan wordplay. There was Father Juan. Then there was The Other Juan. One night at a lonely dinner at a pizzeria I brazenly dropped a note with my number on it into the lap of a curly-haired Frenchman named Jean, The French Juan (aka Jean-Juan). There was The Boring Juan and The New Juan. As the Juans came and went, my new expat friends and I would wax philosophic:

"Another Juan bites the dust," Joe the bitter Brit would say.

"He just wasn't the Juan for me," I'd conclude.

Buenos Aires Ezeiza → San Carlos di Bariloche
   Teniente Luis Candelaria
Departing: *May 14, 2005*

I left Father Juan behind in Buenos Aires for a couple of weeks so I could study Spanish in San Carlos di Bariloche, a resort town on a lake in the mountains of northern Patagonia. I bought the plane ticket reasoning that I really shouldn't miss out on the rest of the country because I was waiting for a phone call from a hot priest who was busy studying for his marketing final.

(Full disclosure: I did invite Juan to come with me. He said he couldn't. I also then paid two hundred dollars to delay my trip for a day, because Juan had said he might possibly take me on a day trip to Tigre, a little delta town up the river with a floating flower and fruit market. He flaked. But then I *totally* left.)

So, alone and disappointed, I went to the mountains of northern Patagonia. I went to Patagonia in very late fall, when, it turns out, no one goes to Patagonia. The sun rose at nine in the morning and set at three in the afternoon. It rained nonstop, too warm by about one degree to snow, and the constant, building-rattling Patagonian winds turned umbrellas (that only dumb American girls attempt to use) immediately inside out.

I was the only student in my Spanish school. The gorgeous Andean mountains that I heard surrounded me were covered in rain clouds. So I spent the first couple of days passing the hours watching the rain fall from one of the town's many warm Swiss-chalet-looking chocolate shops. I took myself to the *parrilla* (barbecue joint) for steaks a couple of times, and read in my guidebook about the wonderful skiing and boating one could do in Bariloche the rest of the year.

Well, hello, Void! How'd you find me way down here?!

And so I asked out my Spanish teacher.

Diego might not have caught my eye had the town not been so deserted. He was tall, and kind, and cute enough. But, more important, he was the *only* thing to do in the place you're supposed to do it. So, after our second day of class, I asked if he wanted to grab a drink.

It was during those two weeks with Diego that I started really speaking Spanish. I can't recommend sleeping with your Spanish teacher highly enough. I moved out of my hotel and into his little room in a charming wood building above a *queso* shop, right on the shores of Nahuel Huapi Lake. We watched the rain fall on the Andes from his little twin bed, an arm's reach from his "kitchen"—a hot plate— and his "half bath"—a toilet underneath a shower head. He kissed body parts, then tested me on the Spanish words for them, obviously. He reported that I was even speaking Spanish in my sleep, which felt like an enormous triumph. He taught me how to conjugate important verbs like *arracanzar*—to come.

Arracanzo, aracanzas, arracanzamos . . .

On our very first date, Diego proved to be a proper Latin lover, not at all too religious for The Deed, which felt great after my departure from the decidedly less infatuated

Father Juan. We took weekend trips around the lake, and walked in Los Arrayanes National Park, a stone's throw from Chile. Diego and I spent a couple of days doing said deed in a hotel room that looked out across the lake in a different direction, at a different part of the Andes, and watched Chile's rain and Argentina's sun make international rainbows. We said they were a metaphor for us, and didn't find that cheesy, like we absolutely should have. We also had some awkward language moments:

"*Que feo,*" Diego sighed one night, amorously. Which means "How ugly."

Most upsettingly, he said this while his face was buried deep in a place that a girl hopes won't ever be called anything but spectacular. My horror subsided when Diego explained to me that *que feo* is an expression Argentinos sometimes use when they mean that something is very, very beautiful. Like saying something is "ridiculous" when it's over-the-top fantastic. Phat instead of fat. He meant *feo* with a *ph*.

Hopefully this is the truth. My vagina is *pheo*. Please don't tell me if you happen to know differently.

Diego told me that he'd just lost eighty pounds. (He told me in kilos, so maybe it was forty, or two hundred, I'm not really sure. The metric system is stupid. But a lot.) So getting hit on by visiting American girls was a new phenomenon for him. We communicated very slowly, very basically, often unsuccessfully. He thought I ate an awful lot of salad and chocolate. He looked at me like he couldn't believe his luck. And he made me feel like I had gotten an A+ in my Patagonian Adventure.

But the most romantic day I had in Bariloche was a day I spent alone.

Up until that day, the prize for "Kristin's Happiest Extended Period of Time Ever" was still held by a blissful two weeks that happened more than ten years earlier. It was at the end of my junior year in college, when I drove across the country with my first love, Vito. We were a few months into our six-year relationship, finally together after our two-year-long will-they-won't-they-Ross-and-Rachel-thing. (That was a timely reference back then.) We were driving my car from Chicago home to Los Angeles, and we took the long way home. It was the first time either of us had driven cross-country, the first time no one in the world knew where we were, the first time we were so completely in love. There were no cell phones and no talking GPS systems, so we could get lost in that great way in which no one will ever get lost again. We read aloud to each other, and dangled our feet out the window, and sang a lot of "Me and Bobby McGee."

"Feelin' good was easy, Lord, when he sang the blues . . ."

We pulled over a couple of times a day to make love, sometimes in front of geysers in Yellowstone or against a tree under Mount Rushmore, while Burgess Meredith narrated a Mount Rushmore movie in the background. (*"Dakota. SOUTH Dakota."*) Sometimes, on particularly deserted stretches of road, we didn't bother to pull over. At night we sat in front of our tent, and drank wine, and somehow knew enough to know that it was amazing that we didn't have any entertainment other than each other, and yet were completely entertained. And I was blissfully, constantly, swoon-inducingly happy.

But I hadn't had such a long, sustained period of bliss since then. I had certainly never been with anyone about whom I was so unambivalent. But even aside from the men of it all, *nothing* had ever been so simple, so 100 percent, so easy. The peaceful moments would come, beautiful, fragile butterflies that would alight for a brief time on my annoyingly restless, neurotic soul, but sooner rather than later there would be a soul itch that needed scratchin', and the sudden movement (and tremendous amount of talking) would cause the happy moments to flitter away. That made me *so* sad—in more than *ten years* I hadn't topped myself. I decided it was because that bliss had been born of a perfect storm of *firsts*, and, at thirty-one, there weren't many firsts left. I figured childbirth was my next shot at that kind of first-time bliss.

But then I went to Argentina.

I realized that Argentina had topped that drive on my first sunny day in Bariloche. Diego was working in the Spanish-school office, and so I was alone as I walked down from his apartment into the sun, and saw that the mountains that had been covered by rain clouds for the last week were suddenly in front of me, and covered in snow. The snow line was just a couple of hundred feet above town, which was still filled with autumn color.

I took a bus out of town to a gondola that went up one of the mountains. There was apparently a rotating restaurant at the top, where one could eat and take in a glorious view of the lake and the snow-covered Andes. I rode up alone, and the view was amazing . . . for about two minutes. Then the lake and the mountains disappeared as my gondola entered a *sopa* of thick white fog. I laughed as I realized that the restaurant at the top of the gondola was sitting in a cloud, and I would be dining to a rotating view of whiteness.

The waiter snapped my photo in front of all that white, as I sat alone in the empty restaurant, eating yet another steak, looking out at the white, well, *void*. I paid the bill and was on my way back to the gondola to ride down, when, suddenly, the clouds parted.

Now I was alone on top of this mountain, with blue sky, the crazy-clear Patagonian sunlight, the sparkling lake, the untrampled fresh snow. I made a snow angel, thinking about the parents and grandparents on both sides who had taught me how to make one long, long ago, back when I was so small that they could hold me out in front of them like a plank and then let go and *poof!* I'd drop into the snow and make a perfect angel imprint. I took a picture of the snow and the lake and the angelic version of me, and then started walking.

I walked for about five hours, in a vaguely downward direction. The snowy trails were covered in a canopy of red and orange and yellow leaves. I walked and walked and walked, no real idea where I was going, just in love with the fact that I was alone on the top of a mountain at the bottom of the world, that I had just gotten on a plane and made this happen. I'd had two months' worth of firsts. I had two dozen new friends from a dozen new countries, and two Argentine lovers. I had learned Spanish, and the tango, and how to buy vegetables in Argentine supermarkets (which is more confusing than you would think). I had learned I was brave. But, most important, I felt just as free and alive and sure of where I was and what I was doing as I had on that car trip, lost in the middle of the country with my first boyfriend. And I was feeling that way *all by myself.* And that made me feel as unambivalent about myself as I had been about my first love.

I had no idea where I was going, but, eventually, I ended up back at the road, and found a bus back to town, and spent a couple more days in Diego's bed that were sexy and warm but weren't nearly as fulfilling or romantic as that unlonely walk alone.

Two weeks into my time in Bariloche, my cousin Emma came down to visit. Simultaneously, I came down with a terrible flu. We decided to treat ourselves to one night in the glorious Llao Llao Hotel. It's a grand old lodge-style place right on the lake, the place where presidents stay when they come to Argentina, and I went straight to bed in the crisp white sheets, while the rain outside finally turned to perfectly white snow. Emma got her own room for safety, and I called Diego, who took an hour-long bus ride from town to take care of me.

Before Diego arrived, I called down and asked for a doctor. They sent a lovely woman who spoke no English, so we struggled through my examination with my broken

Spanish. She wrote me a prescription for antibiotics, and since antibiotics tend, grossly, to lead to yeast infections, I tried to explain that I also wanted the pill that keeps that from happening. She couldn't understand what I was concerned about, but finally understood, and said triumphantly, *"Ahhhh! Infección vaginal ocasionada por hongos!"*

Vagina mushrooms. Actually, literally, vexatious vagina mushrooms. That's what they call it.

Horrified, I nodded as she handed me a pill.

Vagina mushrooms averted, Diego showed up and brought me a stuffed donkey, because my stubborn streak had led to him nicknaming me *"Burra."* (I called him *"Perro Contento"*—Happy Dog—because when he would get particularly excited in bed he had a tic where he would quickly pat me with his hand over and over, like a dog shaking his leg when you scratch his belly.) He spent our last night together nursing me, telling me that he knew I liked him the moment we met, and asking if I believed in love at first sight.

When it was time to leave Patagonia, Diego borrowed a car and took me and Emma to the airport, and after he drove away, texted me:

"Creo que te amo." I think that I love you.

And, because I was about to get on a plane, I shrugged, and texted back:

"Te amo tambien." I love you, too.

Why not? So much easier to say in Spanish.

San Carlos di Bariloche Teniente Luis Candelaria →
Cataratas del Iguazu → Buenos Aires Ezeiza → Los
Angeles International
Departing: May 28, 2005

Emma and I went from Bariloche up to Iguazu Falls, a two-mile-wide expanse of about three hundred waterfalls in the jungle where Brazil, Paraguay, and Argentina meet. It's one of the natural wonders of the world, and the constant roar of the water has the effect of about ten Valium. Local legend has it that the falls were created when a god wanted to marry his human lover, Naipi. But she wanted a life with one of her own kind, and so fled with her mortal lover in a canoe. The god then used lightning to slice the river in front of them, creating the falls and condemning the lovers to an eternity of literally *falling* in love.

We spent a couple of days in the thunder of falling water (and love?), walking over and under and around the falls. We finally took a little open-air train up the river that turned into these awe-inspiring monsters. There is a wooden walkway that goes over the river, and the water is wide, and quiet, and appears to be slow moving ... until it suddenly hits the cliffs that transform it into the huge, mind-blowing phenomenon that it is. We sat over the river, and talked about how the river had become something unique and amazing just by cruising along on its path. How even if your life seemed quiet and typical, you never knew if around the next bend you were about to become something spectacular. Or fall spectacularly in love. We talked about how that was probably how I wanted to feel when I fell in love, like I was going over a waterfall for all eternity, and how that might just possibly not be sustainable, or, if you really thought about it, enjoyable. Then we made fun of ourselves for getting so *deep, man.* Kristin-Adjacent can get pretty cheesy.

Later that day, we sat in the hotel bar and started chatting with two guys who turned out to be fast-talking New York Wall Street types. They asked me what I did, and I told them I was a comedy writer.

"Huh. No offense, but you don't really seem like a comedy writer," one of the guys said. "You seem too mellow. The comedy writers I know are all super loud and fast and frantic." Emma laughed really hard.

Emma and I went back to Buenos Aires for a couple more weeks, and I saw Father Juan a few more times. He took us to a birthday party for two outrageously beautiful twin brothers, and we met his friends, each more gorgeous and well-spoken and well-traveled than the last. But Juan still stood out, for his peacefulness and his quiet sweetness. The partygoers all loved him ferociously and a little protectively, but he was a little on the outside of the boisterous bar scene. He and I sat outside, looking at the boats in the tony waters of Puerto Madero, and he told me about why he had joined the seminary, mostly because of his father's and sister's deaths. Then he took me home, for *mimitos,* and in the morning I sat on my hands to keep from grabbing my camera when he pulled his crisp white shirt over his perfect skin.

Diego would text me constantly from Bariloche, things like, *"Tengo una grande problema con vos."*

I have a big problem with you.

The day before Emma and I finally flew home, Father Juan came over. We walked to the park near my apartment and took pictures of ourselves lying in the grass, Juan smiling as I nibbled on his neck. I cried, talking about what Argentina had meant to me, and he promised that I would be back.

Juan brought me a photo he'd taken of a horse, and a copy of a story about a man who rode a horse from Buenos Aires to Los Angeles at the turn of the century. He was inspired by the story . . . the journey could be made, with the right horse and enough determination. The cities weren't so far apart.

My landlady came to pick up my apartment key, took one look at Juan, and raised her eyebrows.

"You had a *really good trip*," she said, looking steamy.

On the plane, I found a note from Juan on the back of the photo: *"When we are old we will smile about these times we have together when we where young."*

I had changed my return ticket to Los Angeles three times, pushing it back until the very last day before I had to be back at work in the *That '70s Show* writers' room. I thought all of the English at LAX might break my heart, and when

I walked into my house for the first time in months, I burst into tears.

But back in the writers' room, the speed and quality of the conversation were like fireworks. I was still in slow, Kristin-Adjacent mode, and couldn't keep up that first day, so basically just watched the words fly across the room. And . . . it was really fun. It turned out I had missed the linguistic acrobatics of my American life, even if the new "room bit" upon my return from South America was that I was constantly, at any given moment, either in the process of getting impregnated or getting an abortion. (For the record: I've never done either.) The proximity of the two events meant that in the routine I was also getting knocked up by the abortionist a fair number of times. Welcome to comedy-room corporate-speak.

As I came back up to my normal speed, I also fell in love again—with my job, with my coworkers (to comedians, making abortion jokes at your expense is really just a way of expressing love), and with my friends. As much as I loved Argentina, it made me appreciate home in a way that I hadn't before, too. And when I would start to get blue about being in Los Angeles instead of somewhere exotic, I developed some tricks to snap me out of it. I started writing in hotel lobbies, because even though I'm working a few blocks from my house I can pretend I'm on vacation somewhere sexy. I started a routine where I would walk around the city imagining that I was just visiting, trying to see the familiar streets of my hometown through the eyes of a girl on vacation by herself in the exotic city of

Los Angeles, California, U.S.A. It's like when an old married couple imagines their spouse is someone else in bed, spicing things up by pretending they don't belong to each other. The trick almost always gives me that new-love zing for my life, and my city.

I started to dream of a perfect life—not exclusively away from Los Angeles, which I realized my people really made "home"—but one that involved leaving it for a few months a year, so I could have the break that seemed to be required to love it. I also wondered if Juan had been my final fling before I would meet my husband. If the trip to Argentina to prove that I could take on a continent alone was the thing I needed to get to the place where I could merge with someone else again, be half of a whole, and feel good about it. *Maybe that was my last crazy single-girl fun,* I thought as I unpacked my bags.

But that was only the first of my three trips to Argentina.

5

"You Can't
Go en *Casa*
Again"
(Argentina,
Part 2)

Los Angeles International → *Buenos Aires Ezeiza*
Departing: March 9, 2006

It turned out I couldn't get back to Argentina fast enough. The trip had redefined me: I was now the type of woman who gets an apartment in exotic locales by herself for a few months, learns the language, makes dozens of new foreign friends, acquires lovers, and uses the word *lovers*. I spent the nine months between my trips to Argentina starting so many stories with the words "You know, in Argentina..." that people would sarcastically snap things like, "Whaaaat?! You went to Argentina?! Oh my God, I had no idea!"

This new type of woman I had become loved to regale passersby with geographically based dating rules culled from the many miles of road she had seen. So I would trill at cocktail parties how I loved romance abroad because I could abandon my tiresome Stateside need for quick-wittedness in a mate. In a non-English-speaking country, I might chirp, *"I'm* the one who can't keep up with the conversation. Who knows if they're smart or not?! And who cares?! I'm certainly not quick with the German or French or Israeli or Portuguese bon mot, so why should they be?" I'd observe that if I *was* actually in another English-speaking country, where I could, ostensibly, ascertain the smarts and humor of my companion, I'd be too distracted by those *accents* to give a hoot. Accents also, I would add, mysteriously make men seem *older*, which is a handy way of fooling oneself into warming one's lonely hotel bed with an inappropriately young suitor, another no-no for me on home soil.

More often than not, the person at the party hearing this routine would then take a beat, really look at me over their adult beverage, and say something like, "You seem really *good* these days." And I was.

This new, vaguely irritating persona was unfortunate for an incredibly lovely man named Matt, whom I started to date right after I got back. And who probably never had a shot when I had just discovered what it was like to travel alone. But I thought I had gotten something out of my system. That I could somehow redefine myself with an experience that I wouldn't need to repeat. I did, after all, want to find love. And so when I got back from Argentina, I decided to go online, and found Matt.

I fell for Matt right from our six-hour-long first date, where we talked and talked and time flew. But several months into the relationship, after he took in a cat that had adopted me despite the fact that it wouldn't stop peeing in his house, and I met his big, perfect family and took him on his first snowboarding trip, where he broke his wrist on the first run, two things happened. First, my ambivalence reared its ugly head again. *Is he the one, am I irritated a normal amount or more than normal, will I ever love completely, why does he tell me trivia about the director while I'm trying to watch the movie, better make a pro/con list, will I ever meet someone and not feel the need to make a pro/con list blah blah blah.*

But while the ambivalence was familiar, something else also happened this time: spring approached. The time when my work was over, and I could get on a plane and go back to Argentina.

Everything in me rebelled against bringing a boyfriend with me. Argentina was *my place.* Being half of a couple in the place that made me feel so much myself sounded like the saddest thing in the world. Not because I wanted to hook up with handsome strangers, although Father Juan wasn't *not* on my mind. It was because going *alone* was what had made it special. I had even declined to go on Ferris's international New Year's adventure that year, because it was to Argentina. The idea of how much he and his posse would take ownership of the place made me crazy. It was *mine.* The only child in me had never been more terrible at sharing anything than it was at sharing Argentina.

And so, as tortured as I always was when breaking up with a great guy I loved, I broke up with Matt.

"Just not happy, it's not you, there's something wrong with me, I'm just looking for a perfect feeling I'm not feeling, there's nothing to work on . . ."

"You know, Kristin, if 'happy' is your goal, you're probably never going to be happy," my dad often contributed from the couch, over a box of wine. "I shoot for 'content,' which is doable, and then I'm happy."

"Do you maybe think the problem isn't with the guys?" my mother asked, twenty or thirty times. "I really liked that last one."

Anyway, I was single again, and bought my ticket to Buenos Aires. I had stayed in touch with Father Juan, whose e-mails earlier in the year were fantastic, always using the words we had taught each other in bedtime language exchange: "nibbles," "smooches," and *"mimitos"*:

FROM: JUAN
TO: KRISTIN
RE: Te extraño!

You will be remembered as the lovely American that conquered 'los suaves mimitos' of an Argentine.......good things must end but can also be continued..........there were five hundred mimitos left.........for the next time we meet again!!! We'll keep on touch........not the touches of mimitos, nibbles, smooches for the moment, but by this way...jajajaja...I'll miss that ones more! Beso grande!!!!!!

Right?! I had learned in previous correspondence with men in foreign lands that they tend to use exclamation points and ellipses like tween American girls, so I didn't judge him for that. (Kristin-Adjacent is so much less judgy!) Also, what's more fantastic than a "jajajaja"? "Jajajaja" is perhaps the best argument I can think of for taking a Spanish-speaking lover. These adorable e-mails from Juan continued for many months. But when I announced my return trip, there seemed to be a tonal shift.

RE: Loud American Girl Returns

Well, you know that anything you want and I can get for you just make me notice!!!!!!

Hm. Are you noticing the lack of *mimitos* references? The conspicuously absent *"beso grande"*? I was. *But he did use all of those exclamation points, he must be excited to see me again*, I told myself. *Tone is so hard to convey over e-mail.* Of course, I had also stayed in touch with my Patagonian boyfriend, Diego, whose feelings were always much clearer:

RE: BURRA

I miss you so much and every day I think of you......
The truth is that you will always be in my heart. I hope you are well and that you think of me like I think of you. I hope you can come back and do many beautiful things with me. Write me, Burra! I love you!!!!! Write me!!!!!!!!!!

I did not tell Diego I was coming back to Argentina.
Are you noticing a pattern?

After all of the hubbub about going to Argentina alone,
I invited Hope and Sasha along. I wanted to show my favorite girls this place that was so special to me, since only
children like showing off even more than they hate sharing. But they would join me for only the first part of the
trip, so I would still get my romantic solo-traveler fix after
they left. I carefully planned this *Return to Fantasy Island.*
Which, Hervé Villechaize and ABC will tell you, is a dangerous idea.

Here was the plan: Sasha, Hope, and I would rent a
lovely apartment in my old neighborhood in Palermo. All
of my Buenos Aires friends would thrill to my return.
Father Juan would come to the door, take my face in his
hands, and kiss the shit out of me. My best friends would
get to see what all the fuss was about, and I would show
them such an amazing time that they, too, would discover
something new and wonderful about themselves, and fall
hopelessly in love with Argentina, bringing them joy and
us closer. Then they would go home, and I would continue
on to Tierra del Fuego by myself, where I would take a
four-day boat journey around Cape Horn, through the glaciers and penguin colonies just a couple of hundred miles
away from Antarctica, ending up in Punta Arenas, Chile.
I would be a lone woman thinking big thoughts at the
bottom of the world, staring out at the tranquility of the
glacier-strewn ocean, probably an unknowing foreground

in some other tourist's photo, which they might later name *Woman and Ice*. I would then head into South America's version of Yosemite, Torres del Paine, for a few days of wilderness adventures in beautiful hotels on which I would normally not splurge (or reserve ahead of time, which would also turn out to be an important difference). Father Juan would miss me, but I would be back in Buenos Aires for another week at the end of this adventure, where we would fall more madly in love than ever for a few blissful days, before a painful good-bye and a dreamy flight home, which I would spend sipping Malbec and crying deliciously over the impossibility of our love.

That is not what happened.

The trouble started before we even left Los Angeles. Sasha and I had not gone on a girl trip since she had gotten married, and I couldn't wait to get some time with my friend again. But then, a week before we left, her kind, stable, responsible husband came out with a whopper: he had been a secret painkiller addict for eight years and needed to go to rehab. Her husband was a hardworking, successful man who rarely had wine with dinner, and he was possibly the last person from whom you would expect this news. Obviously it was a massive crisis, but since Sasha wouldn't be going to rehab with him, she ultimately decided there was no reason to cancel our trip. So she dropped him off at Betty Ford and we went to Argentina. Needless to say, the mood was off.

Meanwhile, Hope was deep into the longest dry spell I have ever witnessed an attractive person experience. She had been divorced for a couple of years ... and there had been nothing. I mean, there were drunken incidents—an Italian here, a thirty-year-old skateboarder with no car who worked at Sofa U Love there—but they were few and far between, and none ever stuck. This was crazy because Hope had been THE dater of cute boys in high school and college. The ungettable guys all loved her. And she was aging beautifully, her long legs just as coltish as they'd always been. And yet the traffic flow had just stopped. It was mysterious, and heartbreaking.

The only good part of Hope's dry spell was what it meant for our friendship: we were always together. Even though we had been friends since eighth grade, we had never been single adults together before the last couple of years, when her divorce nicely coincided with my singlehood. That was when we went from being friends to being de facto spouses. We called each other husband and wife, because we leaned on each other so completely. We were even great salsa partners (she led, so she was the husband) and slept in the same bed two or three nights a week, depending on which side of town we got drunk on. We bemoaned our revulsion at the idea of the other's vagina, really the only impediment to a lifelong commitment to each other.

Around the time of the Argentina trip, Hope was just emerging from a divorce depression that had, as she put it, "stolen her personality." My friend who traveled around Mexico alone as a twenty-two-year-old girl with just a surfboard, a sleeping bag, and a bus pass, the girl who had been the most consistently ebullient, outgoing, adventurous person I knew, had, for a couple of years, been the quiet girl in the corner, the person I needed to keep track of at a party to make sure she was okay. She took antidepressants for about a year, trying to restart her usually plentiful serotonin, but that, too, led to more dark moments. Like when she got a call from her ex-husband to ask if he could borrow a couple of her pills. Why? Because he and his new girlfriend were going to a rave, and he had heard that taking antidepressants with your Ecstasy helped the comedown.

"You want to take the antidepressants I'm on because of our divorce for your night of drug-induced sex and dancing with your new girlfriend in a club full of people ten years younger than either of you?" she asked.

Reminders like this helped her move on, and, slowly but surely, she had just recently come back to us. I couldn't wait to take her to Argentina.

Sasha and I went down to Buenos Aires a few days before Hope could join. On the plane Sasha's bad luck continued when she came down with a terrible flu, her poor body succumbing to the immense stress it had been under since her husband's "Surprise, I'm a Drug Addict!" announcement. It's hard to talk about exactly how disappointed I was about this, because it rightly makes me sound like a selfish monster. But I was. The trip was already not perfect.

After the long, feverish flight, I got Sasha settled in bed in our apartment in a grand old building around the block from where my apartment had been the year before. It had high, glorious ceilings, and cost next to nothing. I went out into the sunshine to get her medicine and groceries, delighted that I knew where the grocery store was, and that you had to weigh the veggies and get a price sticker in the produce section before you went to check out. The year before, on my first, nervous day in town, I had been an embarrassing, confusing mess with the cashier, who tried to explain to me in Spanish I didn't understand that I was supposed to have done this whole weighing-the-veggies thing, while dozens of annoyed Argentinos waited, and I panicked.

But this year I knew to weigh the veggies. And knowing this small thing about this foreign place gave me a profound joy.

Sasha had a couple of bites to eat and went to bed, telling me that she just needed to sleep, so I should go and have fun. I obeyed. This was a mistake.

While my friend lay alone in bed, sick and worried about whether or not her home life was going to turn into *Requiem for a Dream,* I called Father Juan.

(Now you're thinking to yourself, *Jesus, Kristin, your friend is sick and her husband is in rehab and you're thinking about Father Juan?* Turns out, Sasha was thinking the same thing. And, when I look back, so do I. But at the time, I pushed that thought down deep, somewhere I could pretend it didn't exist at all. It was not a selfless time. Don't worry, there will be repercussions.)

Despite Father Juan's recent nebulous e-mails, I held out hope for a possible *progression* in our relations. He *was* a thirty-one-year-old Latin Man who had been out of the seminary for almost two years after all. Nature is nature. You can keep a sheepherding dog in an apartment in New

York, but it's eventually going to try to herd your dinner guests.

Juan came over to take me out to lunch, and he looked beautiful, and nervous. I had grown out my hair to try to look more like the effortlessly gorgeous, long-haired Argentine girls, and had stopped eating a month earlier, so I hoped he thought the same about me. We walked to a nearby restaurant, and he chatted about his recent college graduation, and his job at an ad agency, while I tried not to sniff his neck or crawl inside his shirt. And then, over *pizza a la parrilla*, he told me that he had a girlfriend. And since Father Juan is not like other Latin Men, it did not need to be said that he was not going to cheat on her.

He gave me this news apologetically, like he was certain I was mostly back in Argentina to see him again, and that this news ruined my trip. I assured him that I was perfectly fine being friends, and that I mostly wanted to see *Argentina* again, since it was *Argentina* that had redefined me, given me a new voice, changed my perspective on the world *blah blah blah*.

That night I made out with a bartender named Oscar. Behind the bar, on the bar, under the bar, after closing time.

Meanwhile, Sasha slept. Whenever I stopped home to check on her, she was asleep. So, after a couple of hours, I would go back out. I reconnected with my expat friends, whose lives were exactly as they had been the year before, and met up with my new naughty-eyed, curly-haired bartender, Oscar, who turned out to have a delightful habit of taking me to parks, removing his shirt, and kissing me in the sun. While this was happening, Sasha was apparently waking up to an empty apartment, and getting sicker, both physically and emotionally, as three or four days went by without talking to her husband, who was detoxing in California. Which sounds a lot more rock-and-roll than it felt. And so, one night, she broke down.

She accused me of abandoning her, and not caring, and being selfish . . . basically all of the things you have been wanting her to say to me. I felt horrible, and guilty, but I was also shocked, because I had offered to take care of her and she had sent me on my way.

"WHO THE FUCK WOULD LISTEN TO ME IN THIS SITUATION?!" Sasha screamed from the kitchen floor, where she was weeping.

That was the moment I learned to ignore people in trouble when they tell you they don't need anything.

This all happened late at night, but I tried to fix it. The truth was, I *had* put my need to re-create my Argentina magic above taking care of my friend, and, deep down, I had known it. I called the expats and got the location of a nearby emergency room, but Sasha walked in, looked around at the filth and poverty and crowds, and turned right back around. We retreated to a cab, where my sick friend had a stroke of genius, and said four magic words to the driver:

"Four Seasons, *por favor.*"

One of my mother's favorite pieces of advice, based on a week she spent in the Singapore Mandarin Oriental with the flu, was that when you find yourself sick in a foreign country, ignore the cost and check yourself into the nicest hotel in town. High-end hotels have doctors on call, room service, and daily clean sheets, and accept credit cards. Since Sasha had basically grown up in my house, she and I had heard this advice from my mom as many times as we had heard her say, "Look both ways before crossing the street," "Nordstrom's has the best shoe sales," and "Always carry twenty bucks for a cab and I.D. so they can identify the body." So we took Sasha to the Four Seasons, checked her in, got her settled in white sheets under a tray of soup, and then she sent me back to our apartment, chastened and feeling like shit.

Meanwhile, Hope was still back in Los Angeles. On the day she was to leave for the trip she discovered that she couldn't find her passport. By the time she got a new one, and got stuck for two strange days in Detroit due to weather and a weird connection, her trip had been chiseled down to about four days. When she finally got to Buenos Aires, Sasha was recovering, but there was still a chill between us, and we needed Hope's energy. Unfortunately, Hope brought the rain with her, and so my attempts at taking my friends around my favorite city were gray and wet, and not as enchanted as I wanted. I was really sad about it.

"Kristin, this always happens. You set your expectations too high for a particular version of perfect and then you get so crazily sad when it isn't," Hope pointed out, for the twentieth time in our lives.

Appropriately, during that week in Buenos Aires, an odd thing was happening on television. A national channel had a twenty-four-hour camera trained on the Perito

Moreno Glacier, which is a huge ice formation in Argentine Patagonia that comes down from the Andes and calves into a gorgeous turquoise lake. The glacier camera never moved, and there was no newscaster speaking. It was just silent twenty-four-hour coverage of this huge wall of ice. Every so often, an enormous hunk would fall, and cause a huge splash, but other than that . . . you were just watching a wall of ice.

I found out that this Glacier Cam broadcast happens every few years. The nature of Perito Moreno is that it advances (one of the world's last glaciers to be doing so, rather than retreating) in such a way that, over the course of between one and four years, it reaches a finger of land and effectively cleaves the lake in half. The two wings of the lake then fight back, slowly melting the stories-high ice from both sides. This two-pronged attack eventually allows the sides of the lake to meet again in the middle, but in the process the lake slowly creates an ice bridge over itself. That bridge then melts and cracks and thins until suddenly, in one majestic moment, the arch is thinned enough that the entire thing cracks, and falls into the lake, creating a splash that is hundreds of feet high.

It was supposed to happen any day, so for this entire week the Glacier Cam was trained on the glacier. Tourists also flock to the region for the "rupture," to sit and stare and hope that they catch it. I found this entire thing very funny, and yet I also found myself turning on the Glacier Cam feed whenever I was back in the apartment. The hope that you would catch the moment was catching.

And it turned out to be incredibly relaxing to just stare at a glacier. Sasha, Hope, and I took to lying in Sasha's big bed at the Four Seasons together, watching it as we fell into an eight p.m. pre-dinner nap, a necessity in the seemingly sleep-free world of Buenos Aires. When a hunk of ice would fall, it was exciting, like a great plot twist in a thriller.

"Whoa! Can you believe the size of that splash?!" one of us would exclaim.

"Awesome. Didn't see that one coming," we would agree.

Ultimately, the bridge fell in the middle of the night, when no one, including the cameras, could see it. The glacier would not perform on command.

One wet, gray night, Sasha went to bed early, still trying to fully recuperate, and my bartender, Oscar, took me and Hope out for a drink. It was Sunday, and most things were closed, but he had a friend who owned a bar named *Sálvame María*—Save me, Mary. It turned out that the "María" was not the Virgin Mary, but Oscar's pudgy male friend Jose-María, who owned and ran the bar. We were the only customers, and I was disappointed I wasn't showing Hope a better time. I needed a great night of South American travel magic, preferably involving romance with a local, and my conscience really needed to deliver something great to at least one of the friends who desperately needed some fun, too.

Oscar tried to do his part for my romance needs right

there on my barstool while María fed Hope approximately as much wine as was probably consumed by the *other* María's son at the Last Supper, but I eventually extricated Oscar's hands from my clothes and the four of us went on a hunt for some fun. The guys took us to a lively Irish bar nearby, where, unfortunately, Oscar, Hope, and I were waved in, but María wasn't. He apparently didn't make the once-over cut. The night looked ready to stall out there, but Hope gamely suggested we all move the party to María's house.

"Are you sure?" I asked her, Oscar's hands in my clothes.

The sweetest wingwoman in the world nodded drunkenly, flashing me a purple-toothed wine smile. "Why not?" And not much later, my dear, dear friend made out with a fat man named María who was not good-looking enough to get into an Irish pub.

It came time for me to go on my solo adventure to Tierra del Fuego. I had introduced Hope and Sasha to Father Juan's brother, Fefe, who was as bad as Father Juan was good, just like in a *telenovela*. But they shared their family's physical genes, at least, and so Hope was delighted to make his acquaintance. Fefe invited Hope and Sasha out to Punta del Este, Uruguay, for a few days, where their family had a beach house. Punta is the beach resort of choice for *porteños*, sort of a Hamptons/South Beach of South America.

Hope and Sasha and I said our good-byes. They hadn't had my experience of Argentina. It hadn't saved them during their times of crisis the way it had saved me. But they hadn't expected it to; only I had. I realized they didn't look at travel the way I looked at it, like medicine, like my chance to right all of the wrongs that might exist in my life. They just had a few interesting days in South America, and went home not too disappointed, but not too changed, either.

I sent them on their way with Fefe, and they were hit with more rain on the beach. It seemed their trip was not destined to succeed. But they apparently played a lot of hands of poker in the casino, and Fefe gave Hope a nice heap of attention, and we do still have a handful of stories from that week we can laugh about. When Sasha went home, she picked up her husband from rehab and got pregnant with her first child a month later, a new life officially begun.

As for me, after my friends left Buenos Aires another travel mishap intervened: I discovered the morning of my flight to Tierra del Fuego that I had left my passport at an Internet café the night before. I discovered this at five a.m., the flight was at eight, the café was not open until nine, there was only one flight a day, which was going to get me to Ushuaia just hours before the one boat of the week would leave . . . Basically, I had to get on that plane, or not go at all. I decided to just see how far I could get.

Buenos Aires Ezeiza → Ushuaia–Malvinas Argentinas
Departing: March 15, 2006

I had a copy of my passport, and so managed to get on the plane that took me to Ushuaia, a little town at the Argentine tip of Tierra del Fuego, but they would not let me on the boat for Chile without the real thing. My big, expensive, carefully planned trip, where I imagined myself as a lonely, romantic figure staring out at the icebergs, was not to be.

So I cried a little, and watched the other passengers load onto the boat, all fifty- to seventysomething couples who would have been my companions on the trip. I then found a liquor store, and a little hostel above town, which happened to be new and clean with heated wood floors for twenty dollars a night, which I knew would attract fun single travelers. I regrouped, drinking beer in the warm upstairs lounge that looked down at the ocean, and up at the glaciers above town.

After a few minutes, three young Israeli guys sat down nearby.

"Grab a glass," I said, holding up my big bottle.

They did, and we shared my beer while we watched my boat literally sail off into the Antarctic sunset, blowing its horn like the Love Boat.

It turned out that the Israelis were fresh out of the military, where one of them had flown F-16s. South America and Southeast Asia are lousy with backpacking Israelis, all having a year or so of low-cost travel fun between their military service and college. Sometimes they get a little "stuck" during this travel time after the army, and the year turns into longer. The Indian, Thai, and Brazilian branches of the Israeli embassies have taken more than one frantic call from the parents of these wayward beachcombers, requesting that they retrieve these nice, stoned Jews and ship them back to their families in the Holy Land.

Anyway, wherever in the world you find these ex-soldiers, they're always up for a good time. So my boat sailed away, and then I went to dinner with my new buddies who couldn't believe I was as old as twenty-eight (I was thirty-two), and then the four of us met a posse of other foreigners who became my travel compadres for a few amazing days.

A brief breakdown of the crowd: first there were the three Israeli pilots. One of them, Avi, had ice-blue eyes, a crazily naughty smile, and, despite the fact that he was built like Kate Moss and was probably too young to legally drink in the U.S., both he and his friends seemed confident that he would be taking me to bed. (In Israel I was told a joke about fighter pilots, and the punch line had something to do with them thinking they could cut diamonds with their penises. So, there's a swagger.) Later in the night we met Alfred, a German hippie mountaineering guide who was taking a few days off from his job in Torres del Paine—the national park in Chile where I was supposed to be. He was as goofy and cheerful as Germans rarely are, with white-guy dreads and a deep joy from getting to sleep indoors for a few days. There was Elizabeth, the tall, blond Australian student/waitress/singer, who was traveling around the world for a year on her own. There were Noa and Eli, a lovely Israeli couple on their post-army trip together, who had met during their tours of duty in the Israeli equivalent of the USO. She sang for the soldiers, and he set up the sound system, and they were the kind of in love that made you want to take pictures of them in the sunset. And, lastly, there was Nick, an adorable blue-eyed science teacher from Maryland who had just come in from a week backpacking alone in the cold wet tundra of Tierra del Fuego, and who, it turned out, was hungry for some warmth and company. But more on him later.

They were all a little younger than I was, and in different places in their lives, but together this crowd saved my trip. The Israeli pilots took me flying, in a tiny little plane over Cape Horn, and our heads smashed into the roof of the plane as the winds tossed it about like a toy. I was still determined to see the penguin colonies, and so the next day I corralled some of the troops to go on a boat trip out to visit them.

It was the year of *March of the Penguins*, and there was no one from anywhere in the world who had not seen the movie and become enthralled with the funny little creatures. We piled onto the boat, which pulled out into the freezing, windy harbor as the fog came in and the rain began to fall horizontally. It was too miserable to stand outside, and the fog made it impossible to see land anyway, so we all found ourselves inside the boat, drinking *cafés cortados* and watching, yes, *March of the Penguins* on the boat's TV system. Dubbed in Spanish.

Just when we had resigned ourselves to the fact that we had flown to the bottom of the world to sail around in the rain rewatching a penguin documentary, the clouds lifted enough that three small islands came into view. And they were covered in thousands of penguins. The thing in the place, at last.

We spent some time watching the hilarious little guys waddle and roll like thousands of tiny Charlie Chaplins, which delighted us all exactly as much as we had hoped it would, then sailed back past seal colonies through a frigid and glorious Antarctic sunset, cool silvers and golds and blues replacing the tropical oranges and reds that seemed to have no place down there.

After the boat ride, we bustled back to our cozy little hostel shivering and windblown, a couple of new Kiwis in tow, to find the lobby filled with music and the smells of food cooking.

"Shabbat shalom!" the Israelis called out.

It was Friday, and the Israeli boys had skipped the penguins and cooked us all a proper Shabbat dinner. We sat down to eat, and they said a quick prayer that was the first Jewish prayer many of the crowd had ever heard, and we ate Argentine steak and grilled veggies and hummus.

Nick the cute American teacher blew in through the door, smelling like rain. He had made a run for beer and ice cream, and pulled up a chair next to me. We talked about his week alone hiking through the rain and wind and tundra. He said he wasn't sure where he was going next.

"Well, I'm heading up to El Calafate and Fitz Roy, if you want to come with," I said, casually. "I could use a hiking buddy who actually knows how to not get lost in the Andes."

"Hm," he said, buttering his bread. "Maybe I'll check into flights."

It was also St. Patrick's Day, which some of the crowd had never celebrated. As an almost 25 percent Irish-American mutt who used to live in Chicago, I took it upon myself to lead a St. Patrick's expedition, and found Dublin's

Irish Pub in Ushuaia, purportedly the world's second-most-southern Irish pub. (The winner is the Galway, also in Ushuaia but half a block south.) I introduced many of my new buddies to their first green beers. We jigged in the pub with some French guys wearing elephant trunks, then moved on and merengued to the Manu Chao album that was constantly on that month in a tiny, ancient fishing-shack-turned-bar until the wee hours of the morning.

Years later, I'd have dinner with Elizabeth the Australian when I visited her hometown of Sydney, and she would come stay with me in Los Angeles, and Avi the sexy Israeli would deliver me from an Israeli beach to the Jordanian border on my trip to Israel. The people I met during those three days in Ushuaia all exchanged love notes for years—*"That St. Patrick's Day was the best day of my yearlong trip . . . You guys were my favorite people I met in South America . . ."*

It was the kind of travel chemistry that doesn't happen all the time, and it all happened because I lost my passport and my plan. If I had gone on the trip I originally booked, I would have been with older, rich, married couples. It was a reminder for me that reinforced my travel rules—don't overplan, and don't book expensive trips if you want to meet fun, single people. The experience also illuminated another fact: regardless of how you travel, as you get deeper into your thirties you might be the only person your age out on the road at all, whether it's in the hostels with the twentysomethings, or on the fancy cruises with the sixtysomethings. In your fourth decade, your compatriots are mostly at home, working, raising humans, getting husbands through rehab, *living for someone besides themselves.*

Suckers. That's what I told myself.

Ushuaia Malvinas Argentinas → *El Calafate International*
Departing: March 18, 2006

Nick decided to come north with me to El Calafate. We said good-bye to our new hungover friends the next day, leaving them to their collective discovery of what comes out of one's body the day after drinking a dozen green beers, and traveled north to the portal town of the famous Perito Moreno Glacier, star of the Glacier Cam. We were a week late for the big movie moment seen by no one, but just missing The Thing You Were Supposed to Do seemed perfect to me on this trip of misses.

Nick and I were a little shy about deciding to travel together, our relationship as yet unclear. When we were confronted with the question of how many rooms we wanted at the hostel in El Calafate, there was a lot of mutual bluster:

"Well, I mean, we can get a double, I guess. Cheaper than two singles," I said "casually," not at all worried about cost.

"Yeah, and it'd be nice to not be in a big dorm room of snoring people," Nick agreed, "not caring either way." "A double, yeah. And . . . I guess . . . two beds?"

"Yes, please, two beds," I agreed, like a "lady."

Of course the only room available had one queen bed.

"Well, if that's the only thing available," I said, happily.

"Yeah, if that's all there is, sure, we can get by with one," Nick agreed, quickly.

We went to our room to change clothes, I noticed that Nick had a smooth, muscled back and flat belly, and then we took ourselves quickly out of the room for yet another steak in town. As we sat in the *parrilla* in front of the room-size fire, where goats were sizzling, each splayed on its own crucifix, we got to know each other better. Nick didn't love being a high school science teacher, yet didn't know what else to do with himself. He knew a lot about mountaineering, but oddly very little about a lot of other topics, topics one would hope the teachers of our children would be knowledgeable about. But he was handsome and sweet, and, it turned out, my knight in shining armor in several ways.

I managed to leave my cash card in an ATM that night, meaning I was now at the bottom of the world with both no passport *and* no way to access cash. It was just one of those trips. Nick said he would take care of me, though, and we agreed that I would cover anything that could be covered with my one remaining credit card, and he would take care of cash needs. I couldn't help but think about my prior magical year in Argentina, which had been absolutely hitch-free. It seemed like God was trying to tell me something, not just about overplanning, but maybe about money, too. I had tried to make this a much more opulent vacation than I ever had before, straying from my history as the girl who "didn't need fancy hotels to have a good time." But all of those opulent plans had blown up, and I had ended up a girl in a hostel who had to borrow money from a near stranger.

Who, granted, was about to sleep in her bed.

Now, was there electric chemistry between me and Nick? Not especially. But, much like with my Patagonian Spanish-teacher boyfriend the year before, there was enough. And in the same way I'd needed Diego to turn a flawed travel situation into a great (unlonely) story, Nick was now on deck.

Nick and I went back to our big bed in our little room, and lay down awkwardly on top of the covers in our clothes. We chatted some more, about how he had been a little disappointed by his experience of trekking around alone—he hoped he wouldn't get as lonely as he had. I told him about the dramatic difference between my two trips to Argentina, and about how I was feeling a little lost and banged up by this one. But I was also kind of peaceful— the message of all of the events, from Father Juan to the less-than-stellar experience with my two best friends to the lost passport and cash card, seemed to be the same one Hope was trying to send me. *You can't control everything. Just enjoy what the world is giving you.* And that message was actually pretty relaxing.

Eventually it got quiet, and Nick and I just lay next to each other, on our backs, staring at the ceiling, waiting to see what was going to happen next. Would we roll over and go to sleep, or do something else? Slowly, strangely, Nick raised the hand closest to me into the air, his elbow still on the bed . . . and just left it up there, his arm at an odd right angle. I looked at his very weird first move, an open palm, a quiet question floating above us, and then reached up and took his hand in mine.

Deal.

We did not just go to sleep.

The next day, holding hands easily now, Nick and I went to Perito Moreno. The sky was blue, the sun was warm, and the air was cold, blowing off the ninety-five-square-mile glacier that could hold the entire city of Buenos Aires. We took a boat along the turquoise lake, and snapped pictures of ourselves kissing in front of the two-hundred-foot-tall wall of ice that, somehow, was advancing forward six feet a day. This three-mile-wide ice mountain was moving a little bit faster than a tree sloth.

Inexplicably, there were flocks of tropically colored parrots in the trees across from the ice, and the green, red, and blue birds against the miles of glacier made us feel like we were in some kind of J. J. Abrams *Lost* universe—polar bears on tropical islands being the clue that you were in another world, or a rule-free TV show. It turns out that if you plan on seeing the glacier fall, it will happen in the middle of the night and you will miss it. But an unexpected trip to that same glacier, days after you theoretically missed the big moment, might lead to a sunny, spectacular day with a new friend, who might kiss you in front of glacial parrots while the ice falls.

After a night in our big, warm bed, Nick and I snuggled through a bus ride to El Chalten, a little mountaineering town at the end of a long, dusty road. El Chalten exists exclusively to service the people who come to climb Mount Fitz Roy, on the border between Chile and Argentina. It's one of the most technically challenging mountains on earth, but Nick and I just took a day hike from town up to the lake at its base, on a rare sunny day, the last day of Patagonian summer. We stood on floating pieces of ice in the lake under the Fitz Roy Glacier, and ate sandwiches in the sun. That night we found a little apartment over a tapas restaurant for about thirty dollars. The smell of baking bread wafted up from the restaurant, and we rattled the one twin bed while the ever-present Patagonian wind rattled the windows.

The next day, we rode the bus back to town, Nick kissed me good-bye, said it had been the best trip of his life, and went back to teaching teenagers in Baltimore.

El Calafate International → Buenos Aires Ezeiza
Departing: March 23, 2006

Back in Buenos Aires, I retrieved my passport from the friend who had rescued it from the Internet café, and had a few last days with my Argentine posse and my bartender, Oscar. I had heard about *telos*, "love hotels" all over Buenos Aires, ranging from the very cheap to the very high end, that could be rented by the hour. It's big business in a country where many people either live with their parents or cheat on their spouses (or both). *Telo* is a *lunfardo* word—the language of the streets of Buenos Aires. *Lunfardo* flips the syllables of normal Spanish words, and was originally a sort of pig latin for criminals, to keep the cops from following their conversations. So an upstanding *hotel* (silent *h* in Spanish) becomes a seedier *telo* in *lunfardo*.

I asked Oscar to take me to one, and he promptly pulled out what was basically a *telo* frequent flyer card attached to a wallet-size list of all of the *telos* broken down by neighborhood. It turned out they were everywhere, on every block. I just had never noticed them because they look like parking garages, for reasons that will become clear.

We drove to one, pulled up to a gate, and stopped the car at what looked like the order window at a McDonald's. But the items on the menu all had to do with types of rooms and hours required—*3 hours of love, only 60 pesos!!!* You could also add on extras like sex toys, video cameras, and drink and food packages. We selected a simple three-hour food-and-vibratorless package, then drove in and up a level, and parked directly in front of the door to our room, which is how *telos* always work. There are never any lobbies, in order to eliminate the possibility of an awkward run-in. Oscar and I walked into our black-walled, mirrored-ceilinged room, and thoroughly enjoyed our bed with a radio built into the headboard. "Your Body Is a Wonderland" was playing, unfortunately, but other than that, it was all I hoped it would be, complete with free toothbrushes and condoms, and a polite phone call five minutes before our time was up.

On my last night in the city, I went out dancing with my friends, and Father Juan came by to say good-bye. I had sent him an update or two over the course of my trip, trying to be "friends," and he had been cordial in return. He came to the party alone, and it was awkward, Juan standing nearby quietly, neither engaging with anyone nor leaving, until I finally just thanked him for coming, hoping he would just go. He got it and left, again apologetically. I kicked myself for sullying our experience together the year before by coming back again. I had replaced the endless ellipses in our relationship with a period. No more possibility, just a final chapter. I thought I'd never see him again.

But I would. You just can't plan these things.

6

"Brazilians Skip Second and Steal Third"

Los Angeles International → Rio de Janeiro Galeão
International
Departing May 2, 2007

I have taken a lot of trips that changed me, that taught me things about myself or the world. *Profound* things.

Nothing profound happened in Brazil.

Brazil was just freaking *fun*. All id, as deep as a puddle. A (married) friend recently described his trip to Brazil thusly:

"You'd be sitting on the beach, and you'd spot the most beautiful woman you'd ever seen. But because the beach was crowded, she'd keep getting blocked ... *by the most beautiful woman you've ever seen.*"

I'm struggling with whether or not to tell some of the

tales from Brazil. I've got images of fathers-in-law and future children reading them, people I would not normally tell. But you know what? If I were a man, I would tell these tales without fear of slut-shaming. These escapades would be laughed off as good old-fashioned oat sowing were I not of the fairer sex, and so I'm going to plow ahead and tell the story of my two Brazilian boyfriends.

They were two of the most beautiful men I have ever seen.

I went to Brazil with my cousin Emma, and we met up with one of the expats from Buenos Aires—the American named Kate. Now, let's talk about Argentina for a moment. It's very close to Brazil. Adjacent, in fact. And after my first trip to Argentina, I had thought of buying an apartment in Buenos Aires (for less than the cost of my car) and going annually. I was dreaming up an idea for a TV show that I hoped I could shoot in Argentina. I had been ready to move there, at least for a while. And, maybe, re-fall in love with Father Juan once his relationship failed, then make beautiful bilingual babies who said *"Hola, mami"* over *medialunas* every morning before I went off to run a hit show in South America. In my fantasy I also started looking a lot like Penélope Cruz.

And yet I wasn't even dropping by Argentina this time. It had been so awkward with Juan the year before, and I had learned my lesson about trying to re-create magic. I was afraid to go back. What if it kept getting worse and worse? Maybe the Argentina magic happened as a result of throwing myself with abandon into a place that was unknown, and I could find the magic again somewhere new.

Brazil.

We started in Rio. You know how all great cities have their important sight-seeing spot? Big Ben in London, the Sydney Opera House? Places of architectural or historic significance that must be seen to have properly "done" the place? Well, in Rio, that must-see spot is Posto Nove, a lifeguard tower on Ipanema Beach. Why is a lifeguard tower the place to see? One reason: the hotness of the people who gather there. Really. This is mentioned in guidebooks.

On Ipanema, different lifeguard towers draw different crowds who gather around them—there are towers for families, gays, dogs, volleyball players, the elderly. Posto Nove—Tower Nine—draws the spectacularly beautiful. And one must remember that the largest percentage of supermodels in the world comes from this region, so a collection of the most spectacularly beautiful of Rio? That's as extreme a category as a gathering of the most diabetic at the Alabama State Fair.

Apparently Posto Nove became the place to be in 1980 because of a man named Fernando Gabeira. As of this writing, he is the current deputy of Rio and was a former socialist activist/guerilla who, in 1969, helped some fellow revolutionaries kidnap the American ambassador to Brazil. In 1980, he returned to Rio from exile in France and was photographed at Posto Nove in the smallest thong you can imagine. He was a political celebrity and outspoken bisexual, but, more important, he looked great in butt floss, and so thereafter Posto Nove became the place to be for revolutionaries (which today means bongo players and pot smokers) and hot people.

The ass is king (or queen) of every beach in Brazil, and, regardless of the size or shape, every woman's swimsuit at Posto Nove was playing hide-and-go-seek up inside its respective tanned, glorious booty. Many of the men were wearing *tsungas*, which are basically man bikini bottoms, and which Brazilians will just go ahead and wear while jogging nearly naked through the city's business district, their phones and keys shoved in next to their parts. Some men played footvolley, an impossible-looking version of beach volleyball using only one's feet, which creates the most impressive physiques we have seen anywhere on the planet.

Emma and I quickly yanked our swimsuits up our rears (important to adhere to local customs) and set up chairs with our cameras and our conspicuously white American asses. We took turns sticking our faces in front of each other's cameras at odd angles, trying to get in photos with these otherworldly-looking people.

"Holy Jesus, get one with him behind me. Quick, he's turning, he's turning!"

"Oh my God, look at that one on the other one's shoulders! Quick! Did you get it?!"

In the same way we'd photographed the giant Christ statue on the hill above town the day before, we snapped shots of the booties, backs, legs, and arms of these frolicking, beautiful people.

"This makes me believe in God way more than that big Christo," my tiny Catholic cousin proclaimed. We lifted our *caipiriñhas* to the Big Man Upstairs.

After a few days of this highbrow cultural tour of Rio, we flew up to Salvador, in the Brazilian state of Bahia, and met up with my expat friend Kate. Kate had been living in Buenos Aires for about seven years, and was a smart, quiet girl whose greatest love in life was her dog, Daisy. Daisy had once eaten several of my personal items during a stay with them, and was generally a wild and unpleasant animal who drove everyone besides Kate insane. Daisy's only redeeming quality came years later, when Kate hired Marco, a very young, very hot *passeaperro*, or dogwalker. He was the only other human in the world who loved Daisy like Kate did, and he eventually became Kate's much-younger boyfriend. Over the years, he tamed Daisy and Kate tamed him, and eventually she moved Marco in, like an old-timey British gentleman might raise and then marry his ward. The three of them have now been together for years, and Kate is four months pregnant. So she basically nailed it.

Anyway, our trip to Brazil happened before Marco came along, and Daisy the dog was still Kate's only true love. Leaving Daisy behind was torture for Kate. She pined for Daisy the way you would pine for a lover or a child. She would come back from checking her e-mail in tears because "Daisy" had written her a note about how much she missed her "mommy." This would upset Kate for an hour or so.

"Daisy said she just stares at my bed all day, wishing I was there," Kate would say, sniffling about the e-mail her well-meaning dogsitter had not realized would decimate her day. "She sounds really upset. I told her that I miss her, too, but I don't think it's going to make her feel any better!"

Emma and I grew to hate that doggy–e-mail–writing dogsitter.

But back to Salvador. The three of us spent a few days in the old city, which is a colorful, crumbling beauty that used to be the capital of Brazil. It was also the port during the slave-trade era, and so Salvador and its environs have the most African influence of any part of Brazil. The food, the way people dance in clubs . . . it all feels African in the richest, spiciest, and sexiest of ways. There are drums in the street, and half-naked people dancing like it's Carnival year-round. Big Mamas in white turbans and long, white dresses serve incredible *moquecas*—spicy coconut curried stews—out of pots over open fires, while impossibly muscled men play capoeira on the cobbled stones. We did it all—sambaed, made new friends, received several offers from Bahian men eager to send us home with Bahian babies in our bellies, got some jewelry ripped off our necks at a *favela* street party—and then Kate sent one last e-mail to her dog and we got on a boat to Tinharé Island.

Tinharé is part of a spectacular archipelago in the state of Bahia. The ocean around the islands is sprinkled with floating oyster cafés, and there are far more palm trees on the white sand beaches than people. The islands prohibit cars, so you'll still see donkeys pulling carts down the beach. When you arrive in Morro de São Paolo, the main town, there are a dozen men in matching golf shirts, all with wheelbarrows painted with the word TAXI. You load your bags or groceries or children into these "taxis," and the men push them behind you as you hike up the hill, down Main Street (a sandy path between two rows of beachfront restaurants and shops), and across the beach to your *pousada*. You don't really ever wear shoes. When it's time for lunch, you walk down the beach until you find a guy with some fish and coconuts, and lie on the sand drinking coconut water while he grills you up some lunch. When it's time for dinner, you just hike your bikini farther up your ass, and go find a restaurant.

Emma, Kate, and I were having dinner on the beach when my first Brazilian boyfriend walked by. The restaurant featured a band of glistening, fat-free men in *tsungas* playing horns and drums, and they were holding a lot of our attention. The Morro restaurants almost never feature drummers wearing pants or shirts, which really should be in any visitor-outreach literature the region produces.

But despite the drum-beating distractions, I still noticed Cristiano. Appearance-wise he fell directly in my sweet spot, with a white-toothed, naughty smile and the coloring of a conquistador. So when he walked by, he caught my eye, he caught me being caught, and he walked right over. This is an almost exclusively foreign phenomenon for me, this summoning strange men with my eyes. Back at home, I'm shy and sort of terrible at *come-hither* eye contact. One time I was walking through a bar in Los Angeles thinking I was shooting some pretty sexy looks all around, and a woman stopped me with a hand on my shoulder:

"Are you all right?" the stranger asked. "You look like you're going to cry."

So I'm not so good at sexy face. Kristin-Adjacent, however, is pretty great at it.

So back to Cristiano. A couple of years earlier, my old crush Ferris Bueller took a posse of people to Rio for New Year's. He told me that a mysterious phenomenon kept happening: he and our equally charismatic male friends would enter a bar, and quickly round up several gorgeous Brazilian women. Having seen this happen all over the world, I feel confident this is how it went. But in Brazil, something strange would occur. After about twenty minutes of happy drinking and flirting, the women would wander off, meet other men, and, within minutes, make out with them. Night after night my American friends would watch this happen, then finally asked a Brazilian woman why she thought they kept striking out.

"Well, had you kissed the girls before they wandered off?" she asked.

"No, we'd only been talking for a few minutes," they said.

The Brazilian girl laughed. In Brazil, if a guy hasn't grabbed you and kissed you within a few minutes, he isn't interested. That's why the girls all moved on.

I could not tell this story to Cristiano, because he didn't speak English. But he still managed to wordlessly confirm that this is indeed how Brazilian men operate. With one addendum: they don't just kiss you. They run the bases right there in public, minutes after meeting you. And another surprise: they don't go in order.

Brazilians are not into boobs. That is the conclusion that my travel partners and I came to after several experiences over the course of our three weeks. As a girl whose boobs have arguably been the star of her physical life, this was a truly foreign experience. Maybe when you live in the country that invented the thong, you spend enough time staring at asses that you forget to look anywhere else. And, as I've said, Brazilian asses, and the confidence with which they are paraded, are indeed glorious. How this comes into play for, say, an American girl making out with a Brazilian conquistador in a beach bar is that within about five minutes, his hands leave her face, bypass the next universally accepted playground, and go straight down her pants. Which is just surprising enough to work.

A brief digression into the notion of "bases." I found being single in my thirties very confusing on a few fronts. How to pace things physically was one of the most perplexing. My mother first introduced me to this conundrum when I was fifteen, and came home unexpectedly to find her and her Mexican-Hungarian boyfriend mid-tussle. After pulling on some clothes, she told me that while I should be waiting until I was older and in love to get physical with boys, she was a grown woman, and so would be exploring some new and exciting things with some new and exciting people. "Grown-ups don't just hold hands," is how she summed it up, which went into the pilot I wrote about her. And she was right—grown-ups don't.

So the dilemma as I saw it was this: as I said earlier, I am not a slut in the United States of America. While Kristin-Adjacent didn't worry much about curtailing home runs, at home I didn't want to sleep with everyone I kissed. Maybe I wanted to get to know the guy better first. Maybe

I was dating multiple people, and I find it too emotionally confusing to sleep with more than one person at a time. So I needed to sometimes say no. And yet it felt ridiculous to be a grown woman drawing lines in the sand of her body. "You can touch me here, but not here" felt just too high school. Not what grown-ups do. So, how to balance these two conflicting needs?

I came up with a new and improved system of bases after a conversation with a gay friend, who had told me that the gay base system is dramatically different from the straight. In his world, first base was a blow job, second was anal, third involved a third, and a home run was pretty complicated but probably involved a swing and a go-go dancer. Obviously these definitions don't apply to every gay man, but the takeaway is certainly that things get very advanced very quickly when women are not involved. Much like with other male-on-male activities, like, say, war, the escalation is fast and furious and often involves bleeding.

(Lesbian bases, I've been told, involve a lot of baths and toys at first and second bases, and buying a house and building a compost garden together as you round third. A home run is when you've stopped having sex altogether and start a book club.)

The gay bases gave me the idea for a new set of bases for grown-up ladies who are struggling with being sexually evolved adults but do not want to become the village bicycle. My new bases involved not which part of your body was being touched with what, but where *geographically* the physical intimacy was taking place. So anything that happened in public, say in a car or on a front porch, was first base, anything that happened inside one's house, on one's couch/kitchen counter/dining-room floor, was second, move into the bedroom and you're at third, sleep over and that's a home run. The system is meaningful, I think, because instead of giving away parts of your body like oranges at mile markers in a marathon, intimacy progresses based on how far into your house and life you want to let your partner get. That seemed like an important distinction.

So, yes, if you want to screw on the front porch, you can still say you stopped at first base. Good, right?

Anyway, Cristiano skipped high school second and went straight to high school third that first night, right there in that beachfront bar. (Which, in Grown-up-Lady Bases, is still just first!) I glanced around, embarrassed, at the hundreds of other people, but they were so focused on getting their own hands down each other's pants that they weren't giving us a second look. Emma and Kate were learning all of the same lessons about base stealing elsewhere in the bar, and it was a small miracle that we ultimately made it back to our hotel without any ballplayers in tow.

I told Cristiano we would be going to another island in the morning if he wanted to come with and maybe fall in love for a few days. He couldn't afford the boat trip, though, and so we said good-bye twenty or thirty times, and then I took his hands out of my pants and went home to my eco resort, like a lady.

———

The next day, the girls and I hopped a little speedboat for Boipeba, an even tinier island nearby. It was off-season, and so when we arrived at the pretty little beach with a few restaurants and inns, we were among only a handful of tourists on the island. We wandered around looking at our housing options, and chose a pretty, brightly painted little set of *pousadas*—cabins—right on the sand.

We spent the day on the beach with many *caipiriñhas*, and then, that night, wandered into "town," which was made up of one main square with four churches around a park. There was a "café" on the square that consisted of four plastic tables and a folding table "bar" in front of someone's house. We stopped for a drink with the three locals who sat out front, and ended up getting a little samba lesson on the quiet square. At one point, I went inside to use the bathroom, and I had to walk through the living room, where a little girl and her grandmother slept on couches in front of the TV.

Relaxed and moving at island speed, we made our way home through the quiet village. And the next morning, I emerged from my mosquito net, walked outside, and found Cristiano in a hammock in front of our room, grinning as he waited for me.

It turns out that Cristiano had a friend with a boat. He hitched a ride to our island, asked the first local where the American girls were staying, and they pointed him in our direction. Apparently even with our bikinis pulled up our butts, we were not blending. For Cristiano's excursion across the ocean to find me, he brought the following items:

1 pair of board shorts (on his body)
1 T-shirt (on his body)
1 pair of flip-flops (on his feet)
3 condoms (in the pocket of his board shorts)
0 dollars

We used the first condom forty-five minutes after I found him in the hammock that morning, on a rock down the beach, in the shade of the trees, as the turquoise waves crashed around us. Like in freaking *From Here to Eternity*, but with better tans and bloodier knees. *Bases? What bases?*

We used the next two condoms after lunch, very aerobically, under the mosquito net in my *pousada*. But we were now faced with our first crisis as a couple: we were out of condoms, which were arguably the glue that was holding our relationship together. Cristiano had no money. And, since for some reason my ATM card was rarely working in Brazil, I didn't either. I had been borrowing cash from my cousin, which meant that Cristiano and I found ourselves knocking on her door, and asking sheepishly:

"Heeeeey. Could we borrow some money for condoms?"

(To be fair, I think I was the only sheepish one. Cristiano was looking pretty proud.)

Emma happily did her part to keep her cousin Bahian-baby-free, and lent me the money for everything Cristiano and I needed that week. As a result, I called her "Sugar

Mama." Cristiano adorably got it wrong, and called her "Mama Sugar," which is what I still call her to this day.

During the day, the girls and I would go on excursions, on horses through the mangroves to even prettier beaches, in canoes through marshes into the interior of the island, and then I'd come back to my island boyfriend, whose manhood wouldn't allow us to pay for him to come along (he was only comfortable with us paying for everything else). He'd spend the day playing soccer on the sand with the local restaurant staffs, and would be waiting on the beach for us to return, smiling and waving as he ran alongside our boat, sort of like a super-sexy golden retriever.

I found out that he was a real estate agent . . . on a fairly uninhabited island. Which might have explained the lack of any money. In bed he was more enthusiasm than skill, but he looked great. And often he would literally throw me over his shoulder and take me into the jungle to have his way with me, which bought him an awful, awful lot.

You may remember that Cristiano did not speak any English, and wonder how we were communicating as we fell more and more deeply in love. Well, we made our way through the week with a sort of Spantuguese we invented, combining our broken Spanish with Portuguese and a dash of charades in a way that worked well enough to do what we needed. He did speak a few words of English, but they were limited to a couple of impressions, like the 007 he did for us one night at dinner:

"The name is James Bond. Bond."

Since he did this with no shirt on, we all applauded wildly. And when we told him it was perfect, we meant it.

After a week with Rich Little, we said *chau*, and the girls and I flew back to Rio for one last night in Brazil. Ferris Bueller had told us to go to Rìo Scenarium, a restaurant/bar/club that he claimed was the best he had ever been to anywhere in the world (I agree). We arrived to find that the line for the club was two blocks long. As we stood near the entrance trying to decide what to do next, a blue-eyed, square-jawed, golden-skinned, broad-shouldered young surfer who was somehow even better-looking than Cristiano looked over, and smiled. In response, I gasped. I might have even said, *"Jesus Christo."* He smiled bigger, and waved us to the front of the line with him and his adorable friend.

This was Rodrigo.

My second Brazilian boyfriend was a big-wave surfer in his late twenties who was just a few days away from moving to Sydney to learn English. Now fluent in Spantuguese-charades after a week with Cristiano, I gave Rodrigo my drink order and he led me through the club, as Emma zeroed in on his curly-haired young friend. The club was a three-level converted antiques shop. There was still a huge array of old, cool stuff everywhere, and there were thousands of gorgeous people of all ages eating, drinking, and dancing. Several varieties of live music poured through every level, from traditional Brazilian music to clubby

DJs, and Rodrigo took me to the first floor, where couples danced to a slow, sexy samba band.

If there is anything more ridiculously sexy than a young, blue-eyed Brazilian surfer who knows how to samba, I just don't know what it is. He pulled me close, and that's when I felt his body. It kind of made my eyes water. Suddenly feeling like a frat boy, all I could think of was how badly I wanted to see him with his shirt off. I've never really understood men's interest in feeling boobs (everywhere but Brazil)—there are no erogenous zones on the palms of one's hands, after all. But all I wanted to do was Tune in Tokyo on Rodrigo's chest, immediately.

As we swayed to the music, and I felt certain that things couldn't ever be better for the rest of my days, Rodrigo leaned close, inhaled my hair, and tried to whisper his first English in my ear:

"You smell bad."

I gasped, and Rodrigo immediately realized his mistake: "Oh, no, good! You smell so good! I make wrong word!" I had to take a minute while I bent over in the middle of the dance floor, holding my belly and laughing, and then, less than twenty-four hours after I said good-bye to my island boyfriend, Rodrigo took my face in his hands.

"I can kiss you?" he said, hopefully.

He got that one right.

Regardless of how I smelled, our night continued on until dawn. Now, again, I had been naked with another man less than twenty-four hours earlier. And, no, I'm not excited that my father is reading this right now. But, for all womankind, and to take a stand against slut-shaming, I'm going to continue. Yes, I was with two men in one day. But, *Dad*, I will say in my defense that there was a (domestic) flight in between them—nearly a thousand miles and close to twenty-four hours—which I feel effectively separates them in a way that feels less, you know, disgusting.

Although *less* disgusting is not the way the rest of this story goes.

Rodrigo took me back to the little two-bedroom apartment he shared with his grandfather, where his baby pictures hung in the hallway. His things were all in boxes for his move to Australia, and there was just a mattress on the floor of his bedroom. The sound of his grandfather's snores drifted through the walls and over we young and not-so-young lovers.

Rodrigo and I took off each other's clothes, and things were just as spectacular as I imagined they would be. All I wanted to do was rub my face on his chest and stomach, and all he wanted to do was flip me upside down so that we could nuzzle each other's genitalia. *Sessenta e nove* is the sexier, Brazilian way to say it. Now, I was a guest in this country, and my mother taught me to eat what is being served, but I've always found this move to be in the "more-is-less" department. Do you focus on the giving or the receiving? In my opinion, both suffer.

But there I was, on top of Rodrigo in his grandpa's house, exchanging pleasantries with the lights on (my idea, due to my interest in seeing him, which I was now regretting given the view one has in this particular position). After a few minutes, I tried to flip around for the Main Act, but Rodrigo held me securely in place, still enjoying the overture, apparently. I'm sure Freud would have some things to say about Rodrigo, as from the feel of things he seemed to have a desire to crawl back into the womb, face-first. Which was not unpainful. A couple of "Ows" might have popped out of me as the young surfer tried to dive into me much like I imagine he dove into a wave. My repeated attempts to flip around were repeatedly rebuffed, so eventually I gave up and just let the guy attempt to split me in half.

Eventually, in not a small amount of pain, I righted my ship, and faced my new close friend. And that's when I noticed what looked like a scratch mark on his nose, covered in a bit of blood.

"Oh, no, did I scratch you?!" I said, kissing his nose.

"No! Is from you!" Rodrigo chirped.

I gasped. I *bled* on his nose? It was not that week.

"Is your ass!" Rodrigo said, as cheerful as a Mouseketeer.

It was not my ass, but it was certainly Ass-Adjacent. The boy had torn me open, and I had bled on his face. And he was thrilled about it.

Oh, Brazil.

A couple of weeks after we got home, I got an e-mail from my island boyfriend, Cristiano:

RE: TUDO BEM?

TUDO bom!!!!! I find money for fly to Los Angeles!!!!! I stay with you????? You can pay for three weeks food and party?????

The man from the carless island without a dollar to his name had found the money to fly to Los Angeles. But the nice thing about not being twenty-one is that you know what happens if you ship them home. Inviting a penniless Brazilian into your house for food and parties is like inviting in a vampire, but with more drum circles. Once they're in, you're powerless and they're not going anywhere. And, as was the case with my other Brazilian, they may very well draw blood.

I told Cristiano I would love to see him if he made it to Los Angeles, but that I couldn't help him with the food and parties. And I never heard from him again.

So, here is why I really want to tell this story, despite some shame: Brazil was fantastic. Was it sordid and revolting? Yes. Am I horrified that my father is reading about it? Tremendously. Would I recommend the exact same experience to even my very own daughter someday? If she spends as much of her life worrying and overanalyzing as her mother does, absolutely. Everybody needs a little bit of *that's crazy*, a little bit of *way too much. Balance, Dad, like you said.*

So, the deep and profound moral of this trip? If at all possible, at least once (or twice) in your life, get as naked as possible with a Brazilian.

Oh, Brazil.

7

"Dominican
Surgeons Are
Not Half Bad"

Los Angeles International → La Republica
*   Dominicana, Aeropuerto Internacional General*
*   Gregorio Luperón*
Departing: December 26, 2007

2007 was the year I had emergency surgery in an island nation and sex with a Finn, in that order.

Ferris's New Year's trip in 2007 was to the Dominican Republic, and it fell smack-dab in the middle of the hundred-day-long Writers Guild of America strike. The strike was just and necessary; TV and film writers were not getting paid when our work was aired on the Internet, and, soon, the kids told us, no one would be watching TV or movies anywhere else. When you work in a career that has the same average lifespan as a professional athlete's, you want to make sure you're getting paid. Those dollars have to last for a lot of years after one is deemed too old to write dick jokes. So we struck against the companies who were telling us that they weren't making a dime off the Internet, while telling their shareholders (publicly, and in writing) that profits were through the roof because of the Internet.

Despite the just cause, things on the picket lines could get awkward. Other unions would come out to picket with us in support—teamsters, nurses, airport workers. So . . . people with *real* jobs. People with the kinds of jobs where you sometimes had to do things like, well, stand up. And who made way, way, way less than writers do. So there were days spent marching hand in hand with The People, united against The Man, before heading to The Palm for lump crab meat, steaks, and martinis. Or sometimes we slummed it and went to have free food at a nearby diner where Drew Carey ran a tab for striking writers. The postpicketing conversation was invariably about how much more exercise we were all getting on the picket lines than we had during our days spent gorging on free food in a writers' room.

Gross. We know. But that's what happened.

At work that year, I had been operating under what is called an "overall deal." What this means is you are paid a lump sum to work on shows for your studio, as well as develop original shows for them (which you then shop to the networks). I had sold the studio an idea for a show that was basically *Cheers* in an expat bar in Buenos Aires (all in the hopes of getting to shoot it there), but the networks all balked at a show set in another country. Americans, they feared, wouldn't relate to people who wanted to do something as crazy as leave America.

As part of the deal, I was also working on a sitcom produced by the Farrelly Brothers, the guys responsible for movies like *There's Something About Mary*. Because it was a Farrelly Brothers show, in the pilot, the lead got ass-raped by his date's pet monkey. This meant days in a writers' room where my talented, serious boss would shake his head and say things like, "I don't know, you guys, I just don't think we have the monkey-ass-rape moment of this episode yet." And so we would hunker down and try harder.

That show only made it six episodes, and my expat show hadn't sold, so I was not exactly "working" for a living when the strike hit and made me stop working.

You can see why the nurses and truck drivers should have hated us.

As for my personal life, I had spent the year going on a *lot* of first dates. There were a few months spent with an overly emotional French writer, who absolutely made it into my Top Three in the bed department, but who called his own writing "beautiful." He would call late at night, tortured, wanting to make a confession:

"Tonight I feel like an emotional vampire."

I did not know what that meant, but we still talked about it for two or three hours. There was also an unfortunate crying hand-job incident. (I was giving the hand job, he was crying.) Again, though, when he wasn't crying, Top Three. I called him "Frenchie Summer 2007" because we met on the Fourth of July, and I had promised my friends I wouldn't keep him past the equinox. I extended the relationship for a couple of weeks into the fall for previously explained reasons, and then he was gone.

But other than Frenchie Summer 2007, they were coming and going pretty rapidly. There was a charming, guitar-playing development executive for a couple of months before we realized we were just supposed to be friends, an Israeli landscaper whom I fought with and kissed at the dinner table on our first date (in that order), and a tall, heavily muscled capoeira instructor I called the Black David (à la Michelangelo), whose body in my white-tiled shower will be seared into my mind until the day I die.

While the relationships did not blossom into love, all of these experiences were really yielding fruit in my career. That monkey-ass-rape show was about newly divorced people going on terrible dates. The year before, I had written on *How I Met Your Mother*, another show about missed romantic connections. And I found that, in both instances, I had some stories to contribute. Stories I couldn't have contributed just a few years earlier. A lot of them. Like, maybe enough already. Remember when Robin went to Argentina and brought back a hot Argentine on *How I Met Your Mother*? That's a trip paying for itself.

Meanwhile, Sasha had just had her first baby, making the wildest child in my life now officially a mother, and on to a different life, while I was still amassing stories with my husband, Hope. I realized my life was changing when I called myself a "serial monogamist" to my friend Dan, part of the Ferris Bueller posse who had only met me at thirty, *after* my decade spent entirely with two long-term boyfriends.

"What are you talking about? You're not a serial monogamist. You're always single," Dan said, laughing.

I'm not sure why this was news to me. I was a long way from my three-guys-at-age-thirty days. And a lot of my new friends, the ones with whom I was running around the world, hadn't even known that other me.

Another thing happened in 2007: I went back to therapy, and started taking antidepressants. In Los Angeles, this news is exactly as odd and interesting as saying you started eating three times a day, but since I know this isn't quite as everyday in the rest of the world, I'll explain. (Or perhaps by this point in the book, you're not at all in need of an explanation, and are instead reacting to this news with an exasperated, *"Finally."*)

In any case, the therapy and the antidepressants sprang out of a trip I took in November, just after my monkey-ass-rape show went down and my pilot didn't sell. I met up with Hope for Thanksgiving in Spain, where she had been working for a week before I arrived in Madrid. A few hours after I got in, we went out for dinner, waited for our table for two hours at the bar, then had another bottle of wine once we finally sat down, and then took the party to a club, where I danced with a man who assured me he was a toreador. Jetlagged and not at all sleepy, I wanted to pursue this information further, but Hope ran out of energy, and so we took our drunk selves home at about four in the morning.

She collapsed in bed, but I was still wide-awake. I'm

normally a marathon sleeper, but I always travel with Ambien for long flights and those first couple of nights of jetlag. So I popped a sleeping pill, and sat, drunk, at my computer while I waited for it to kick in.

It kicked in.

In the morning, I would discover that I had e-mailed just about every man who had ever touched my body or soul. I even jumped on my Match.com account to e-mail a few who might do so one day in the future. At first, the e-mails were just drunken, typo-filled notes that looked like they had been written by a cat. But eventually, clearly, the Ambien kicked in, and that's when the correspondence got upsetting. Here is a partial list of what I wrote:

To Matt, the boyfriend I broke up with in between my trips to Argentina, I wrote a huge amount of upsetting "miss you" stuff, which boiled down to asking if it all would have worked out if only his penis had not been so big.

To Oscar, the Argentine bartender: filthy stuff. Just ... yeah. Filthy.

To Frenchie Summer 2007: very sexy, cat-typoed suggestions that also turned a little angry.

To an Asian guy on Match.com:

You seem suuuuuuuupercool, but unnfortunately i'm just not atttracted to Asians. i know that sounds horrible, I swear i'm not racist, I date *every other race,* just sadlyy never Asian.

Horrifying. Even more horrifying, years later, I would of course meet this guy. A friend of a friend. Super-attractive, super-cool, totally remembered being bummed out by our correspondence, I'm a dick.

And there were more! To a few other random guys who had not called me after date one or two or three, I sent more anger, with progressively more typos.

And then, worst of all, even worse than Asian racism, I wrote to Ben:

> Didm i makee the bigggest mistake omy life breaking up with you? Do youthink we could have been aa family by noow? Ilove you, you're beautifulll and iwonder.

In the morning, I woke up with a gasp. I ran to my computer and groaned with progressive volume as I read what Ambien-fueled Kristin-Adjacent had done, and then quickly wrote about a dozen more e-mails: *rescind, rescind, rescind! Ambien! Madrid! Sorry!* The recipients were all very gracious, the Asian guy even offering to still go out with me. But Ben's was ominous:

> No worries. But we should probably talk about this when you get home.

Years later, I would start hearing stories of other people who stayed awake and wrote on Ambien. And everyone used the same words to describe what they wrote: *angry* and *sexual.* This is apparently an Ambien thing, just like sleep eating and sleep shopping. But I didn't know that at the time, and I felt *horrible* about all of these messages. And also, for the entire Spanish trip, disturbed. What was all of this anger that came out of me? And this love for Ben? I had rejected him for *years*, and yet this is what came out of me when drugs and alcohol could knock down my walls? What kind of enormous, messed-up walls were in me if these were my real feelings, but I didn't at all want to act on them in the sober light of day?

And so, a little freaked out, I went home, went back to therapy, and started taking antidepressants. I started talking about why I was so terrified of really, truly connecting with a man, of needing someone the way you need someone when you build a life with them. We talked about my relationship with my father, with whom I'd had my strongest parental relationship because I grew up with a constantly working mom, and who had then disappeared from my life completely for four years when I was nineteen.

That story is a long one, but here are the highlights: My dad had married my stepmother with three days' notice when I was seventeen. The marriage came out of the blue, because for the prior two years they had been dating, she had told him she only wanted to marry a doctor. I didn't go to the wedding for a variety of reasons, but mostly because I thought my dad was marrying this materialistic woman primarily out of fear of being alone.

While my parents' divorce had at first been amicable, when my stepmother came into the picture she forbade my dad from ever seeing my mom, and limited his contact with her to phone calls about me. I spent my high school graduation searching the crowd for my father, who she had made sure wasn't there. When I decided to go to Northwestern, my stepmother made it clear she thought I was being selfish and spoiled. She gave me a lecture about how she knew plenty of people with houses and boats who didn't even go to college, let alone a private university far from their family. My parents had put aside money for college for me when they divorced that covered my first two years of school, but when my junior year was upon us, and the tuition had to start coming out of everyone's pockets, and all of that coincided with the birth of the first of my three half-siblings, my stepmother did not like it. I suddenly found that my father's visits to bring my new baby sister to see me were getting cancelled, and, one day, that my father's phone number had been changed, and I was not given the new one. The next day my mother was served with papers: my father was suing her to get out of paying his half of my tuition. He and my stepmother followed their attorney's advice and slandered my mom in the suit, I flew home from college to testify on behalf of my mother, she won, and my father and I didn't speak for four years. His parents cut me off, too—the Bible says to honor thy mother and thy father, after all, and I was apparently not doing what Jesus would do if Joseph sued Mary.

After this first big, childhood-ending heartbreak, I dove headfirst into my relationship with my college boyfriend, Vito, hastily filling the hole left by my father. Over the years when my dad and I weren't speaking, I would write long, multipage rants to my father, furious that he wasn't fighting for me, that he wasn't coming to get me. He would respond with simple cards that only read "I love you," which did a great job of rendering those words almost meaningless. Five years later, I would lose Vito in the same *"Sure I love you but sometimes shit happens"* way I lost my father, and my belief that true love doesn't last was reinforced nicely.

The therapist did not think I had let go of any of that yet.

Eventually, just before Christmas, I went out to coffee with Ben, who wanted to talk about what was obviously still between us. I started crying immediately upon seeing him, and told him that the lovey Madrid e-mail had just come from the Ambien and, perhaps, from depression and fear. I was working on the depression and fear thing, but I did not want to get back together. I told him I wrote lots of e-mails to lots of people.

It was not cool. That would come back to bite me in the ass.

Not unrelated to my decision with Ben, I was also back in contact with the now single Father Juan. Let's remember that Juan lived a continent away, which, as per my issues previously discussed, worked *great* for me. After some friendly "no hard feelings" e-mails about our awkward time in Buenos Aires, he had invited me to meet him on a trip to Peru he would be taking solo, just after New Year's Eve, where he proposed we climb up to Machu Picchu together. But Father Juan was hard to read, and I feared he was inviting me as a friend, which I feared would lead to massive disappointment and depression on top of a very, very tall cliff. Or maybe we'd finally have sex and fall in love. The possibilities were extreme.

I was trying to decide whether or not to join Juan in Peru when I went on Ferris's New Year's trip to the Dominican Republic. It was two months into the strike, and about thirty people (many of them striking writers) rented three properties on the sand, nestled prettily between a windsurfer beach and what turned out to be a brothel filled with teenaged Dominican prostitutes serving elderly Russians. A lovely family of five ran our bed-and-breakfast, and the family's sixteen-year-old daughter seemed interested in starting a little side business that involved procuring one of my thirty- and fortysomething male friends for her own use. Apparently lots of girls in town had these much older international "boyfriends," who brought their wallets to visit a few times a year.

We did not stay on the right side of the island. We learned this one day when we were taken to the other side of the island by one of the girls in our group, a hilarious fourth-generation Palm Beach aristocrat who was weirder than the rest of her family, and so hung out with us. She put the thirty of us on a bus and drove to the other side of the island to visit her sister's "property," or what might more rightly be described as her sister's landgrab.

Her sister and her husband had just led a coalition of American investors to buy a twenty-two-hundred-acre plot of Dominican land that included a resort, a five-star golf course, hundreds of acres of virgin jungle, and miles of beach that had been on a Best Beaches in the World list. They bought this piece of property from the government of the Dominican Republic because the president decided selling one of his country's ecological jewels was worth the money. Their vision for the green, perfect place on the white-sand beach was "updated Athenian village." A *New Yorker* article on the project explained this as a place "in which four-star restaurants and art galleries could share street space with locally-run fish shacks and pool halls." Moby and Charlie Rose were also investors. There was going to be an "artists' colony."

Needless to say, the property was spectacular. And while we felt much like, well, colonizers who had stolen the land of the natives, we had a lovely day golfing and being fed picnics on linen-covered tabletops that truckloads of help quickly set up on the spotless sand. Then we came back to our low-rent side of the island, where the beaches were developed, covered in trash, and inhabited by, mostly, Dominican hookers, navy guys visiting brothels, and Russian guys visiting brothels.

I spent a few days debating what I should do once the trip was over—go with some friends to Cuba, or jump on a plane for Peru and Father Juan. It turned out I would do neither. On the morning of December 31, a group of us piled into a car to go climb some nearby waterfalls. My friend Will was driving. He pulled over, I stepped out of the car, he didn't know I had stepped out, and then he decided to repark because he always parks twice because he's got what could be called OCD or, at the very least, an extreme case of "worrywart." Anyway, he reparked on top of my foot.

"Back up back up back up!" I screamed.

Mercifully, he stopped before the car rolled all the way over me, which would have crushed my ankle and leg and perhaps severed a major artery that was about half an inch from where my injury was, and which the doctors later explained might have caused me to bleed to death. So, we luckily avoided all of that, but when he backed up, my bare foot was still smashed into the broken asphalt. *Degloved* is the word the doctors used to describe what happened, which meant I basically tore off the flesh on the bottom of my heel, down to the bone. I degloved my foot.

As soon as the wheel rolled off me, I took a brief look. People later described what my foot looked like as "a shark bite." The next time I would get up the nerve to look at my right foot would be about four weeks later. In that moment, I just lay back in the car and started to cry. One friend got in next to me, and held my bleeding foot out the car window.

"It's okay, it's really not that bad," he assured me.

Two little Dominican girls walked by, glanced at my foot, and screamed.

An hour's drive and two small-town health clinics later, I ended up having surgery to put the bottom of my foot back on. Mercifully, my husband, Hope, was by my side, as always. And she had lived in South America for two years, so spoke fluent Spanish. So she could translate as I wept and screamed things like, "No, God, they have to stop, please tell them to stop!" as the nurses tried, over and over again, to get an IV into my vein. The twentieth time was the charm.

IV finally in, I lay in pre-op in the Dominican hospital, listening to the waves crashing and the local baseball game outside the open window. I asked Hope what was going to happen if I needed a blood transfusion here, on the same island as *Haiti*. That sounded like a bad idea.

"Well, what blood type are you? Maybe I could give blood," Hope suggested helpfully.

"Hm," I said dubiously. "I don't know about that."

"Are you saying you feel safer getting blood from the country with one of the highest HIV rates in the world than you feel getting blood from me?" she demanded. I shrugged. She started laughing. We then spent some time wondering which of the thirty close friends currently on the island had blood that one might be willing to inject into one's own body.

"Will's girlfriend is pretty young," I said. "Less time out there filthing up. Maybe her."

Luckily, I did not need a blood transfusion, just forty or so stitches inside and out, and a warning from the doctor that the skin was so mangled that I might still need a skin graft when I got home. Mysteriously, my rusty Spanish turned into fluent Spanish under anesthesia, and so orderlies, nurses, and amused assorted workers were gathered around my hospital bed when I woke up apparently telling absolutely filthy jokes in fast, easy Spanish. Will filmed it. He also has footage of my foot bleeding in the street, and some photos taken later that night of him, in a car, looking sheepish as he pretended to drive over a life-size cardboard cutout of Hervé Villechaize that inexplicably came with us on all of these New Year's trips.

The doctors wanted to keep me overnight, but it was New Year's Eve, and the thought of a night in the hospital alone, or with a sad friend I'd made miss out on a party, was too much to bear. And so Hope, always my savior, catered to my pathological need for fun and broke me out of the hospital for a New Year's Eve on many painkillers. She threw a gold shirt on me, and my fantastic friends took turns carrying me around, making me feel like a crippled, drugged-out princess. Lindsay Lohan might get that every night, but it was pretty special for me.

For our New Year's party, we took over an open-air restaurant where we made a couple of new Finnish friends: the host of *Finnish Idol*, with the Seacrest frosted tips and waxed chest and all, and his friend Levi, a professional on-line poker player who was traveling around the world indefinitely. Rachel Dratch was on the trip with us, and they were especially excited about "Debbie Downer." I wish you could hear two blond Finns try to do that bit.

My friends decorated my cast, nestling a champagne bottle top on my big toe, and danced on tables around me, sprinkling glitter on my drugged-out head. There was the annual celebratory strip down to the gold man bikini by my friend Thomas. Nice boys carried me to the bathroom, and nice girls gave me attention and champagne, and the sixteen-year-old girl from our B and B dirty-danced with one of my thirty-five-year-old friends. Ferris danced with his Parisian girlfriend, whom he had flown in for the occasion, and my secret crushes continued not to lead to midnight kisses. I finally gave in to the events of the day and went home around one, as the party raged on.

The next couple of days were a haze of intense heat and excruciating pain next to an ocean I couldn't get into. I finally called my doctor stepdad, and found out the "pain-killers" I had been given were really just extra-strength Tylenol. Hope then spent her day driving around the island like a trouper to find me the good stuff, and then I happily propped my foot up on a lounge chair poolside, and hung my head and arms over the side of the pool into the cool water. I read *Eat Pray Love*, which caused me intense stress due to how much I both hated the narrator for her self-involved, self-inflicted misery in the middle of a pretty amazing life, and deeply related to her, due to my tendency to be self-involved and inflict misery on myself in the middle of my pretty amazing life.

On our last night in the D.R., we had a bonfire on the beach, and the Finns were invited. I was getting pretty good on my crutches, and, if I may be so bold, the poker player noticed. Much like the lion might notice the limping ibex. Meanwhile, the ibex noticed the lion right back. *Boy, being a limping ibex sure is exhausting. Maybe getting devoured wouldn't be so bad.* Now that I was not recovering from general anesthesia, I could focus on what was important: Levi was a six-foot-four, white-blond, blue-eyed Viking. He was a rainbow of pastels, sort of the color of an infant's bedroom, but in a hot way. He looked squeaky-clean, like he would smell like a cool, northern, ocean wind.

My future Finnish lover sat down next to me, and we talked about our lives. He apparently won enough online poker that he just lived all over the world, in hotels, on a constant vacation. He had been in the Caribbean for months, and was considering where to go next. I waxed poetic about Argentina for a while, like always, and then he carried me down to the sand for the bonfire, fetched me a drink, and hauled an enormous log over so I could elevate my cast. And there we sat for eight more hours.

Our bonfire turned into a talent show under the stars. There was a lot of talent around that fire, and so the show was fairly amazing. People sang, and joked, and danced, and Levi and I snuggled close, my cast propped up on the log. When it came time for Levi's talent, he sang an old Finnish folk song about a fairy in a northern wood. He sang it beautifully, and, if my decision had not already been made the first or second time he carried me into the bathroom like I was a tiny kitten, it was certainly made once he started singing about Nordic Sprites.

The party ended abruptly when our fourteen- and sixteen-year-old Dominican host girls joined the bonfire. At first they were lovely audience members. But then they wanted to show us their talent. *Adorable!* The sisters got a guy with a guitar to play an acoustic version of some booty song, and did a dance for us that one normally only sees on an elevated stage, with a pole. It was when the teenagers were on all fours with their backs arched that everyone decided it was time to break the party up.

But Levi and I stayed by the fire for a few more hours, watching the constellations move across the sky. Eventually sand started getting in awkward places, and so he carried me upstairs, and appointed himself in a way that would have made his pillaging ancestors proud, and which I wholeheartedly felt I deserved. The most revolting, rewarding, Viking-esque highlight occurred at the end of our time together, when Levi's Thor-size special moment exploded out of him with such velocity and pizzazz that it ended up all over the headboard, and the curtains, and the walls, and, finally, on my Viking's own pink face. If you've ever watched those news shows where they go into a hotel room with a black light to show that the room is covered floor to ceiling in bodily fluids, and you've wondered how that could have possibly happened, I can tell you: there was a Viking in that room.

But he kept my foot elevated the whole time.

I went home in a wheelchair, my friends all happily "taking care of me" when it came time to go to the front of the holiday airport security lines with the cripple. Will gave me his first-class plane ticket, like the gentleman he always is. I didn't need a skin graft, but my foot took two months to heal. It's hard to feel more single than when you live alone and are on crutches and can't even get yourself a glass of water. I spent the first week at home with my ecstatic mom, whom I appreciated as never before as she happily cooked and fussed.

"I'm so happy you're here!" she gushed. "At your age the only way I'll get you in my house for this long is if you get injured. Or maybe someday if you get married and are having problems," she added optimistically. For once, I agreed. I couldn't believe how good it felt to be taken care of by someone I could take from without guilt. I found myself snuggling into her lap on the couch, like when I was little. She got to rest her head on my chest for the first time in a decade, which caused her to declare that part of her wanted to die before I had children so that she could come back as my baby. I didn't find this creepy, like I absolutely should have. When I finally left my mom, and went home to the house in which I was usually perfectly fine being alone, I cried.

During that time the writers' strike raged on, and my overall deal was "force majeured," which means it was terminated because I "broke my contract" by not showing up to work. It also meant losing a year's income, in what would have been the biggest financial year I'd ever had. Levi wrote a few weeks later that he had been inspired by my stories about Argentina, and was weary of the beach. He ended up moving that month to Buenos Aires, where he bought three apartments with his poker winnings, and where he lives to this day.

And Father Juan had a great time in Machu Picchu . . . without me. But we were back in touch . . .

8

"Frodo Is the Hottest Guy in New Zealand"

Los Angeles International → Auckland Airport
Departing: November 12, 2008

There is a man shortage in New Zealand. That's what my *Lonely Planet New Zealand* guidebook told me as I opened it for the first time while my plane lifted off the tarmac for my solo trip to blow off steam in New Zealand.

I was running away from home, again. One might even say that this time I was sprinting. But this time it wasn't because of romance, or a need for personal growth. This time it was because of Hollywood.

Earlier in the year, while waiting for my degloved foot to heal from Dominican surgery, I wrote a sitcom about my family. It was an unusual thing for me to do, writing. That may sound strange for a writer, but I had been employed on a long-running show for years, and never seemed to find the time or energy to write anything but what I was being paid to write. While other writers might spend their nights and weekends writing their novels, or their screenplays, I spent my nights and weekends playing. (And sleeping. I need a tremendous amount of sleep. It's my least favorite thing about myself.) And, every spring, when others might really dig into their own passion projects, I got on a plane.

Depending on my mood and level of self-loathing, I had two explanations for this. If I was on an emotionally healthy upswing, I said this was because I was just following my father's most consistent life-advice: *find balance.* All work or all play is no way to live. *Plus,* I'd say while surfing Expedia, I needed to get out there and "live" if I was going to have anything interesting to write about. On the other hand, if it was a blacker day, I used the whole not-writing thing as evidence that I wasn't a "real writer"—"real writers" being people who wake up in the morning and grab pen and paper like they're bread and water.

(I don't define "real writers" like this anymore, mostly because of a compulsive writing-procrastination habit of mine—collecting stories of great writers who hated writing. If you're a writer, I highly suggest this incredibly soothing pastime, as it turns out it's almost all of them.)

Anyway, being hobbled during the writers' strike limited my options: I couldn't work. I couldn't picket. I couldn't get on a plane. And so, for the two months that it took the open wound on my heel to heal, I actually wrote something.

The show was about half autobiographical. There was a

terminally single thirtysomething girl at the middle of it. Familiar. But *this* girl's problem was that she was so busy taking care of her parents and their lives that she was ignoring her own. Not familiar. Now, years of incorporating semiautobiographical details into scripts had caused me to notice a pattern: network executives almost always zero in on the autobiographical parts and end up saying something like, *"When the character does that, I just don't find her all that likable."* This is why so many writers are in therapy. Even though you tell yourself all great characters are flawed, and that TV executives just want everyone to be cheerful vanilla people who are, for some reason, always, *always*, good at their jobs, deep down you are a crazy neurotic writer type motivated almost exclusively by your need to be liked, and so you grind on it when people don't like a character who is so very obviously *you*. I once worked on a show where the main character was a hopeless romantic, modeled after the show's creator. During the successful show's first season, both the audience and the network gave feedback that this character was a "pussy"—more romantic than any straight man would ever be. Stung by the criticism, the show's creator "butched up" his TV version of himself. Even more interesting, though, he started to adjust his own romantic behavior, becoming more of a player, more of a "cool guy." It was a fascinating thing to watch, this art imitating life that then changed because of the criticism of the art.

So, the "me" in my pilot got a little cleaned up.

My parents got the TV treatment as well, but in the

other direction. Because you've gotta root for our selfless girl at the center, you see, as she faces down an army of crazy! So my classy, married, well-spoken mother got turned into a fast-talking, man-eating corporate star who was still single and living a much sexier life than her daughter. My father was a little closer to his real self—a sweet, easygoing, boxed-wine-drinking couch potato who had a second round of kids at a late age whom he parented with an excruciatingly hands-off style. In the pilot, his wife has left him, and our girl is busily co-parenting her own half-siblings with her father. In real life, my stepmother was still married to my father, and I saw my three little half-siblings (who were now seven, thirteen, and fifteen) every two or three months.

When you create sitcom characters, you need to figure out two things: what their flaws are that make them funny, and what their special talents are that make them lovable, so that people want to spend half an hour with these people in their house every week. Think of the racist Archie Bunker, who you nonetheless loved like your own father. As you'd imagine, coming up with your parents' flaws is not difficult. But what I found wonderful was how easy it was to come up with what was special about them as well. The process of writing all of us, even in an only partially accurate way, was the most therapeutic thing I'd ever done. Years of actual therapy had helped me understand my family better, but hadn't really made a dent in the amount my parents could drive me crazy. But writing the pilot did. My dad and stepmother and I had moved past the lawsuit and four-year estrangement a few years earlier, but I still had lingering resentment toward them for causing the first and biggest heartbreak of my life. Writing the pilot somehow finished all of that off.

(It also helped my relationship with my mom to honor her only request: that the actress playing her be thin. When we were discussing Kirstie Alley for the role she was weeping and having a lot of nightmares.)

The truly remarkable thing about all of this was that the pilot was a success. During the course of the strike, the networks dumped most of the hundreds of pilots they had commissioned before the strike started. So almost none were being made that year. And yet, in this impossible year, in the middle of an almost dead sitcom market, once the strike ended, a big, fancy network decided to make mine. Statistically, this was a miracle. I told myself that *this* was the reason my foot had been run over in a third-world island nation! So I would be forced to sit still, *in the void*, and write this show, which would cause me to find peace with my crazy family, learn to trust my writing abilities, and acquire fame and fortune.

We shot the pilot, and I cast my family as extras in the scenes with the actors who were playing them. My dad showed up to set coincidentally wearing the exact outfit I had my actor dad wearing for the scene (Hawaiian shirt, cargo shorts, outdoor slippers). The shooting process was not smooth, but in the end, the pilot tested through the roof.

The network president was unhappy with parts of the pilot, but his executives all made a big play for my show, and, miraculously, against all odds, we got an order for twelve more episodes. But, again, he wasn't happy with the pilot, and wanted rewrites and reshoots. No problem, I thought! We can do that! I hired writers, we wrote ten more scripts, we built three stages full of sets, and the new episodes seemed to write themselves. The show felt alive and organic; the magic was there. But then I would get a call from the network, saying that the president still wasn't happy with the twentieth, or thirtieth, rewrite of the pilot that everyone else loved.

When people ask me what it was like to have my own network TV show, I describe it like this: it's like spending your day going back and forth between two rooms. In one room, you have just won the lottery. All of your loved ones are there showering you with praise and love, and you are handed a huge check in front of a big banner that says "YOU DID IT!" while a triumphant brass band plays and confetti falls from the ceiling. But then you are yanked out of that room, and put into a second, dark room, where gray-faced angry people, perhaps lit from below like in a Kubrick film, scream, "YOUR BABY HAS CANCER AND IT'S ALL YOUR FAULT!!!" The girl who was mean to you in high school (she's there, too) then adds, "BECAUSE YOU'RE AN UNTALENTED WHORE WHOSE HUGE THIGHS RUB TOGETHER WHEN SHE WALKS!!!" Then you get to go back into the first room . . . for a few minutes.

Repeat. For six months.

In the 2012–13 television season, at least two show-runners I know of had to leave their shows in the middle because of nervous breakdowns, and a third committed suicide. So by comparison I did okay: my worst day as a showrunner was when I accidentally pooped my pants, which was how I learned why my fancy office had a remote-controlled door and private shower.

Ultimately, days before shooting episode two, as Ohio was called for Obama and the confetti fell on his beautiful family on that stage in Chicago while I popped Tums, my show was shut down before we even got to try. The thing that had felt meant to be was not meant to be. Hundreds of people were out of work, and it was all anyone in the city wanted to talk to me about. And while shows fail 99.9 percent of the time, and so you go into this business expecting it, my show failed at a point in the process that was very unusual. Usually, the network doesn't let you shoot the pilot at all, or they do but then don't pick up the pilot to series, or they air your show but the ratings are bad so you get cancelled after a few episodes. But getting cancelled after the show's been picked up, but before shooting or airing anything that could prove that we were indeed doing good work . . . that was a sucker punch. It felt like I had really, personally, blown it.

So on the day my show was cancelled, like some people run to church or a bottle, I ran to Expedia.

Three days later I found myself with my Lonely Planet book, drinking on a transpacific flight heading away from Hollywood, learning that Kiwi men share my need to run away from home. That's why there is a shortage—so many of them go on walkabout for so long that they find women in other countries, marry them, and never return. Which sounded like kind of a great idea if I had only been traveling to a country with enough men to go around.

I landed, and went straight to the home of a high school friend who was living with his Kiwi wife about forty-five minutes outside Auckland, in sheep country. I hadn't seen my friend Josh for years, and we had lost touch. But when I was desperately trying to think of where I should run to, I remembered that Josh lived in New Zealand, which sounded like the perfect combination of far and exotic yet safe and easy. So I shot him an e-mail asking if I could land at his house for a few days while I licked my wounds and got my bearings, and he immediately said yes.

I had only met his wife, Olivia, once before, at their wedding seven years earlier. They had gotten married in San Francisco on a trolley pulled up next to a park that was hosting a needle-exchange program, several months after they met at a rave at around ten in the morning. A few months after the night/morning when they met, they found themselves climbing a tree, and, when they got to the top, Olivia proposed.

"It just seemed like the thing people do," Olivia said.

A few months later, they were married by a club-kid friend of theirs who had gotten ordained online, and who shakily read the ceremony off the back of one of those plastic-windowed envelopes. Josh wore a tux that was a little too big, and Olivia wore a high-necked, thrift-store, old-timey lace wedding dress, and so the tiny blond bride and groom looked like kids playing dress-up. Someone's dog cut its paw and jumped on Olivia, so there was a bit of dog blood on the front of her gown. For her footwear, the bride chose a black rubber river sandal.

Now happily ensconced in a little house in sheep-covered countryside, Olivia and Josh were all smiles and good vibes. Their equally happy dog loped through snout-high wildflowers toward me when I arrived at their green, blooming place, and my mood immediately lifted. We went hiking that first day, and brainstormed fun things for me to do in New Zealand. Olivia suggested a silent meditation retreat near the black sand beach where they shot *The Piano*. Her friend had recently spent ten days there, not reading, not writing, not exercising . . .

"So, what do you do for ten days?" I asked Olivia.

"You just sit and be *silent*."

Now, you may remember some of my issues with silence. So this idea resonated like a gong. *Silence*. Might that be *exactly* what I needed? The argument could certainly be made that at least 25 percent of what had gone down with my show could be blamed on my mouth. What I had said to whom, and the varying degrees of politicking I had managed and mismanaged, had certainly been part of the show's downfall. I had been an open book to untrustworthy people, and that had been my undoing. And it was not the first time my prolific lip-flapping had gotten me into trouble in my life, professionally or personally.

I had even had medical problems as a result of my mouth. For years I'd been losing my voice. On a good day people said I had a sexy, Demi Moore sort of timbre, but after a night out it was absolutely more post-op Kathleen

Turner. I ignored it for years, but finally was losing my voice entirely so often that I went to a doctor to find out it was basically the result of every kind of nodule and nighttime acid reflux and allergy you could think of that would attack one's vocal cords.

But the doctor emphasized that my hoarseness was also caused by a more pressing problem—*my personality*. His main advice was just to *talk less*. Which had only been my unaccomplished New Year's resolution for thirty or so years. Oh, and there was also this nugget from him, given to me while he fed a camera up my nose and down my throat, with regard to sleeping with my cat, which was adding to the problem:

"Try to get something with two legs into your bed instead of four."

"*I TYING!*" I had protested, while choking on the camera.

In addition to finding love, getting rid of my pet, and changing my personality, I was supposed to stop eating and drinking basically everything that gives life meaning. So . . . I was hoarse. And walking through the hills of New Zealand wondering if all signs in my life were pointing to me shutting up for a little while.

What would ten days of not speaking even feel like? Almost immediately, my fantasy about the silent meditation retreat started to include a handsome, silent stranger sitting across the meditation yurt. We would spend ten days communicating with *only our eyes*, falling deeper and deeper in love without speaking a word. Even without speaking, I would *just know* that he loved children and dancing. He would *just know* that I was neither a morning nor a night person, and would think being at one's best only between ten a.m. and seven p.m. was normal and charming. And at the end of the ten days, a bell would ring signaling the completion of our vow of silence, and he would walk up to me, and say:

"*Hello.*"

"*Hello,*" I'd reply, taking his hand.

And we would be in love.

I was so enamored with that ending that I immediately started writing a play with that "Hello" as the last line. (*In my head* I wrote it. Let's not get excited and think I actually put pen to paper.) That final "Hello" before the stage lights went out would leave the audience wondering—would they really be in love once they found out that the other person was nothing like they imagined, like the audience had known all along? *What if this play was a huge hit?! I could marry my meditation boyfriend and become a playwright and move to New York and be done with Hollywood forever!!! And, by the way, FUCK that network president who didn't even give me a chance to prove him wrong!!! I should have just picked up the phone months ago, and told him that—*

So that was a no on the silent meditation retreat. I would have adventures and find international love instead, I decided. Which, really, is the only way I've ever found to quiet my mind, if not my mouth.

Quiet country life with Josh and Olivia was not leading to either adventure or love, but I had one other contact in New Zealand. A friend who worked in extreme sports connected me with her "hot Maori friend" who sold surf and snowboard gear, and he invited me to come stay in Mount Maunganui, a little beach town on the North Island. Josh offered to drive me there, and when we arrived we found that the hot Maori wouldn't be around until the next day, since he had gone away for the weekend . . . with his girlfriend. So Josh and I got hotel rooms and went out to dinner.

We ended up meeting a posse of fun Kiwis who invited us back to a house party right on the beach. The party was very cool, with a bonfire on the sand, a DJ, and lovely, friendly surf people dancing everywhere. *Oh, hello, international sexy love story.* But *everyone* was coupled up. And very into gardening. The biggest, hottest Maori surfers would amble up, lean in close, and shout over the pumping electronica in those adorable accents:

"My sweet peas are going *off* right now! The boys came over and we put up a new deck and trellis, and the vines are loving it! They're doing so well my partner and I are thinking of expanding the veggies this year if we can move the compost heap," one might offer, except in a twenty-minute version, with his girlfriend suddenly appearing on his lap.

And then another huge dude would start to talk about his tomatoes. For an hour. They *love* their gardens in New Zealand.

There is something about New Zealand that attracts runaways. Over and over and over again, other travelers told me their stories. And almost no one was just there to see the scenery. Everyone was going through something, running away from something, processing something, putting off something. I learned that night in Mount Maunganui that my sweet, cheerful friend Josh had moved to the country in New Zealand after ten years in San Francisco because of a nasty little speed habit he had acquired as a result of the fifteen-hour workdays of a chef. He couldn't quite figure out how to stop, but thought removing himself to a green, quiet place at the bottom of the world might do it. He was right.

The hot Maori and his lovely blond girlfriend invited me to stay for as long as I liked. This is what all Kiwis do, inexplicably. When I was ready to move on after a few days, they took the day off work to drive me to Rotorua, an actively volcanic national park like Yellowstone with crazy stinky weird stuff coming out of the earth. With the funky smells of Rotorua returned the emotional funk of my work heartbreak in Hollywood, my first-week running-away high fading as my new friends drove off. So I kept moving.

My Mount Maunganui friends insisted that I go to Queenstown, a mountain town on a lake on the South Island, where bungee jumping and canyoneering and just about every other extreme sport were invented. They e-mailed their "gorgeous" friend Alex, who lived in town, and promised I'd be shown a great time. Why I expected Alex to be a hot, single, interested, male extreme-sports guide, after so much evidence that this was not going to happen on this trip, is beyond me, but I did. As you would expect, because you are brighter than I, Alex was a beautiful, thirtysomething woman. And instead of meeting me for a beer, like I suggested, she met me at the airport, with my name on a sign, then took me back to her lovely two-bedroom cottage on a flowery hill overlooking the town and the lake.

"I hope this is okay," Alex said, as she showed me to her extra bedroom, where she had put lavender on the pillow. "Stay as long as you like."

This is just what happens in New Zealand. In the six weeks I ended up spending in that country, originally knowing only one local, I paid for a place to stay for exactly seven nights. Kiwis just kept passing me to other Kiwis, who inexplicably would invite me to stay for months if I wanted, and then call another Kiwi down the road to take me in if I was moving on. Maybe being in the middle of the ocean at the bottom of the world makes them happy for a visitor and a story, or maybe they're just the most hospitable people on earth. As someone who comes from a group of friends who no longer give each other rides to the airport or help each other move, I found it remarkable.

Gorgeous Alex turned out to know every extreme-sports guide in town. That first day, she and I went down to the lakefront and lay in the sun, watching paragliders float down from a mountain above us. I said I'd love to paraglide while I was in town.

"Easy! That's Casey flying down right now. I'll text him," Alex said, and pulled out her phone. Moments later, smiley, adorable Casey dropped out of the sky and landed lightly on the sand in front of us.

"Welcome to town, American friend! Got your text,

done for the day, but I'll take you flying in the morning," Casey trilled in his delightful accent, almost as he landed. He then threw his parachute into a backpack and invited us to come across the street to the bar where the flyboys were all gathered for postwork beers, a parachute under every barstool.

That night I extended my trip by three weeks.

But I would not end up kissing any of these men, regardless of how long I stayed. I would go on glorious, wind-whipped rides around the lake on the back of their Ducatis, and blast through canyons on their speedboats, and eat and drink in their homemade houses. I would hear stories of how the idea of bungee jumping came to two of them one night on acid, twenty years before, and of their famous illegal leap off the Eiffel Tower that brought bungee jumping to the world stage. I would go to a couple of memorial parties/flights with them (an alarming percentage of their population had died in extreme-sports accidents, and they always memorialized these victims with more extreme sports). I went to one flirty (taken) flyboy's fortieth birthday, which was out in the country, at the base of a mountain, at the paragliding headquarters. While a hundred people danced on a deck under the stars, he and a few friends took their parachutes up to the mountain above us at midnight, and flew through the pitch-black night to the dancing throngs way below. Their headlamps glittered faintly in the sky above the makeshift dance floor where we all watched them drift down through the darkness for half an hour, until they finally landed perfectly in the middle of the party.

While there were not a lot of handsome men in New Zealand (too small a genetic pool of Brits breeding with Brits?), the few there were lived in Queenstown. But they all had girlfriends. Perhaps another result of being on a sparsely populated, male-deficient set of islands at the bottom of the world—the cute ones are hunted too aggressively to roam free for long.

Finally, on yet another day that Casey and the other Kiwi flyers said was too windy to go safely, a twenty-year-old Swiss paraglider named Swiss Dave offered to take me flying. And because my fear of missing out on a nice heartbreak-numbing adventure is far greater than my fear of getting blown into a mountain, I went.

Swiss Dave and I drove way down the valley, to a launch spot he said was safer on windy days than the mountain above town, where the pesky buildings and large freezing lake could make a missed landing a bummer. We drove up a mountain, he strapped me to his chest, and we ran off a cliff, floating into the sky over the green, green valley. It made me feel like Supergirl, and Swiss Dave started doing tricks, spiraling to the right, and then to the left. I loved it . . . until I started to get nauseated.

"I think I don't feel well!" I shouted into the wind.

"Yeah, it's rough up here!" Dave shouted back. "Probably was too windy after all. Gonna miss the landing spot!"

"I kinda think I'm gonna be sick!" I finally confessed, as we kept drifting.

"We're almost there. There's a sheep field that the farmer lets me land in when I overshoot. Hang on!"

Finally, fifteen seconds before landing, I could hang on

no longer. For some reason I decided that when one needs to vomit while falling from the sky strapped to the chest of a Swiss man, the best move is to cover one's mouth with one's hands. Which did a great job of making sure all of the vomit went back onto my own face, as well as around my head and onto the face of Swiss Dave. This all happened about four seconds before we hit the ground, hard, and I fell face-first into a pile of sheep shit, Swiss Dave on top of me.

"Nice!" he exclaimed.

I met up with Swiss Dave five years later, in Interlaken, Switzerland, where he was living. He was still paragliding, and Emma and I were traveling through after a spring snowboarding mission on the Matterhorn. I bought him a beer, and apologized once again for my gastric faux pas all those years earlier. He waved me off—it apparently happens all the time.

"What percentage of the people you take up puke on you?" I asked him that night, in a loud Swiss basement nightclub, as he danced behind my cousin.

"About eighty," he admitted, grinning. "At least one per day."

I finally left Queenstown. The uninterested and/or coupled-up cute boys were getting depressing. I started to wonder if my romantic luck abroad was limited to non-English-speaking countries, where my personality couldn't get in the way. My gloom began to return, and I would e-mail my writer friends and my producing partners from my show, and ask what I could have done differently to keep it all from imploding. The answer was always the same: *nothing*. It was doomed politically from the start. But I couldn't stop replaying notes calls with executives, conversations with actors, moments that I mentally rewrote until I was smarter or more political or more manipulative or less trusting than I had actually been.

One thing was for sure: I was not yet ready to go back to Hollywood.

I needed to walk. So I joined a five-day hut-to-hut hiking tour of the Milford Track, one of the iconic Great Walks of New Zealand. We walked eight to ten hours a day, through green, wet valleys, sometimes in the rain, always surrounded by dozens of waterfalls streaming down the black mountains on either side. At night we slept under down comforters in secluded lodges that were only for the walkers, and ate three-course meals with wine we didn't have to carry on our exhausted backs. I spent the walking days alternating between peaceful and angry. Sometimes just breathing in the green, sometimes playing out various drafts of perfectly written "so there!"s against those who did me wrong in Hollywood as I marched.

My walking mates, mostly other solo travelers, were, for the most part, no less tortured. Among the group, we had:

One punk-rock-haired Australian girl who was going through her first divorce at twenty-six.

One twentysomething Swedish student whose mother

had kidnapped her and her siblings as children. Her mother then brainwashed them with lies about their Canadian father, who died before my friend finally found out the truth and tracked him down.

One sixty-year-old Australian owner of an online gambling site who had just lost his mother.

One fortysomething American couple and their single female friend, who struggled valiantly not to be sad about being a third wheel.

One thirty-year-old, muscled Texan who had just cashed out of a successful sex toy business and was trying to figure out what to do next.

And finally there were two fiftysomething Kiwi businessmen, old, jolly friends who took hiking and fishing trips together a few times a year, and whose wives and grown children were friends back home. One night, in one of the cozy little lodges, I watched the two buddies rubbing each other's sore backs and feet . . . and heads and legs and chests. Further conversation made it clear that these quarterly fishing and hiking vacations were also vacations from their marriages, and heterosexuality.

"Do your wives know?" I asked them.

"Probably," they said cheerily. "Who knows. But we don't talk about it."

"Have you ever thought of leaving them, and being together?" I asked.

"Nah, the girls are lovely. And the four of us have a nice time together. We just like a little *Brokeback* variety!" one explained. They had been taking these trips for almost thirty years.

We all walked, and talked, and sometimes separated and spent the whole day walking alone. The scenery looked like that of *The Lord of the Rings*, and we felt like explorers on a quest. I started replaying the last year of my life less, and started to think about the future more. At night in the lodge, my new friends reported the same phenomenon. Divorces were becoming less important, deaths less tragic and more a part of life, ideas for "what's next" springing up with each step. My "tragedy" felt much less like a tragedy in the face of these real tragedies, and more like what it was: a really lucky experience that just didn't last forever.

Our five-day walk ended in Milford Sound, a spectacular bay surrounded by dramatic fjords, on a dark, stormy day. We celebrated the journey, dancing in the outpost's one pub, and playing pool, and taking pictures of one another in big group hugs. I held off an inappropriately young kayaking guide or two so I could just chat and laugh with my new friends. I had finally taken the universe's hint: this trip was not for kissing boys.

(To this day, many years after my New Zealand adventure, I have one sad, lone condom in my toiletry bag. It made that trip to New Zealand with me . . . and came home with me. Six years later, it's become sort of a good-luck totem, that hopeful condom that never got used, but is extraordinarily well-traveled.)

Jana the kidnapped Swedish girl had been traveling around New Zealand on a bicycle. She had ridden alone, with all of her belongings, across the South Island, over a mountain range, staying with sheep farmers along the way who would call their friends who were a day's ride down the road to make sure she had another bed for the next night. She and I decided to travel together for a few days after Milford, and so got a little car, and headed east to Kaikoura.

Kaikoura is a tiny town on the water, famous for its marine life. I had grown up on the ocean, had traveled to dozens of beach towns around the world, and yet had never seen a whale. It was weird, and I was determined to see one here. Jana decided she'd rather see wine country, and so we separated for the afternoon.

You could go whale watching two ways: on a boat, or in a helicopter. Since in New Zealand only two vessels of any sort are allowed to be near a whale at any one time, once a whale surfaces it's a race by all of the tour companies to be one of those two. So the helicopter is the way to go, because you get to the whale first. I learned in the hostel that my ability to take the more expensive helicopter option made me a "flash-packer" in this part of the world, which basically means you are a backpacker who can afford private rooms in the hostel and helicopter rides. I liked that—it sounded age-appropriate, but still fun.

I went up in the helicopter after a day of swimming in the ocean with hundreds of wild dolphins. We were instructed that if we sang to them it would get their attention, so a dozen of us floated in the frigid Antarctic water singing "Hot Cross Buns" and "Paradise City" into our snorkels. The dolphins swam by with their babies, who nosed me in the tummy and jumped over and under us as they passed. After the dolphin swim, I headed for the helicopter, where my tour partners were a gorgeous honeymooning couple from, of course, Argentina. The man could have been Father Juan's brother, all shiny hair and *dulce de leche* skin. We went up together, and I got to see my first whale in the wild.

I ended the day alone on a black-sand beach under a glacier-covered mountain, and as I watched the sun set, I noticed something: I wasn't mentally fighting with anyone in Hollywood anymore. I was just alone on a beach, and at peace. The year started to coalesce for me: I had basically gone to grad school for showrunning. I knew how to do it now. I had been given an amazing experience, and a four-million-dollar short film about my family. I had learned I *was* a real writer, that if I had to write a new script in one day every day for months for forty-five bosses with conflicting directives, I could. What had been the worst part of the show experience was how out of control I was. But getting on a plane and getting away from it all gave me my life back so I could see what was ultimately a work failure as just a small part of a big picture of goodness. My life as it had lain out so far felt very full, and rich.

But also, I realized ... *done.* Not like I was ready to die, or change careers, or leave L.A. forever, but I realized at the end of this day of spectacular experiences by myself that I had *a lot* of days full of spectacular experiences by myself. The whole Lone Woman at the Bottom of the World thing was pretty checked off. Perhaps, finally, even played out. Just as I had proved to myself that I was a real writer, I had proved to myself that I could be happy and brave and tackle the planet by myself. So . . . I didn't need to prove anything anymore. I could stop.

I was ready to stop doing all of this alone.

I said good-bye to Jana, spent another couple of weeks driving around alone (on the wrong side of the car, and the wrong side of the road, feeling like Superwoman), taking kayak trips (with an all-female group, natch), and going to Peter Jackson's Christmas party with a hundred nerdy American visual-effects guys (my life at home). I slept in haunted, empty hotels at the end of long, rainy roads, lonely and spooked; I slept on a houseboat hostel in the captain's (captainless) quarters; I slept in the homes of new, lovely Kiwi friends-of-friends-of-friends-of-friends. I had so many adventures with so many kind, hospitable souls that my faith in upright primates was restored.

And since that was the real goal, just in time for Christmas, I packed up my unused, well-traveled condom, and I went home.

9

"Thirty-Five Is Too Old to Be Sleeping in a Bathroom"

Los Angeles International → Brisbane Airport
Departing: April 3, 2009

There are moments in one's life that make one realize one could be making better choices. That moment for me was when I found myself, at age thirty-five, sleeping on a bathroom floor in Australia. For a week.

When I came home from New Zealand, I was a new woman. I felt wise and washed clean by the highs and lows of the previous year. I was ready to create and be loved and grow up. I went straight to my agent the day after I got home and told him I was taking the year off from TV to write my first movie. I had Christmas with my family, and then drove up to Mammoth with Hope and some other friends to snowboard for a few days on our way up to a twenties masquerade New Year's Eve ball that Ferris and Thomas were throwing in an art deco mansion in San Francisco. I felt great.

And then, an hour after we drove into Mammoth, I walked out of a restaurant, slipped on black ice, and broke my leg. The same one that had been run over 360 days before.

Once again, my husband, Hope, took me to the hospital. The next day. After she went snowboarding. There were ten feet of fresh powder and blue skies that day, and I would have done the same thing.

As I lay on the couch waiting for my friends to get off the mountain, I got even more philosophical. God really, *really* wanted me to sit still in the void. The small hints were not reaching me, so he was resorting to physical violence. But . . . the void is so *lonely*! So I put off the void-sitting until right after I flew home from Mammoth, saw a doctor to make sure I didn't need surgery, hitched a ride up to San Francisco for the masquerade ball, and Lindy-Hopped all night in my air cast.

But then, *after that*, I definitely sat still in the void for a full couple of weeks. I couldn't drive so I found myself back at my mom's, who couldn't believe her luck. Her daughter hobbled and in her home two years in a row! Her dreams were coming true.

But . . . *voids*. Right? So right in the middle of this big one, I went out to dinner with Ben.

Remember Ben? The guy I was dating when I crushed on imaginary Ferris five years earlier, the heart I broke when I was not yet ready to settle down? Well, he was finally over me. That had been a process since the Ambien e-mail debacle two years earlier, but he had done it.

And then there I was, literally tenderized like pounded meat by my year of work, failure, and physical and emotional battering. My New Zealand beach realization that I was ready for all of the things I had feared I was too broken to ever want felt both good because it meant that I was normal, but also terrifying. *I was normal.* Years later, Lena Dunham's character on *Girls* would have a similar moment when she broke down and wept to a nice, handsome doctor with a beautiful house, "Please don't tell anyone this, but I want to be happy . . . I want all the things everyone wants." I was embarrassed to be a thirty-five-year-old woman who was looking for true love, and a family. It was so freaking *typical.* But I was also deeply relieved that I'd finally gotten there.

And so, in this place, I reached out to Ben, and asked him out to dinner, as friends. He was not all that into the idea, since he rightly felt I had not acted in a particularly friendly way over the last few years. I guess that had been hanging over me—Ben was the person my internal *mishegas* had hurt the most. I wanted to fix the relationship, build something from this new place of peace.

At dinner he had a new swagger from a new job and a new band and, apparently, a new plethora of women. He also just had a new *certain something.* Probably that *certain something* was that he was over me. And so I couldn't stop thinking about him.

In retrospect, going back to Ben was probably an attempt to prove to myself that *I had been fixed*. In a scientific experiment, you keep one thing constant when you're trying to figure out which combination of elements is the right one. Ben was the constant. There had been love there, but I had ruined it. If I could go back to the original source and build love there again, the only logical conclusion was that *I* was now working.

After a couple of months of soul-searching and obsessing, and talking to friends who insisted that Ben and I were not a match and that I had broken up with him for a reason, I finally decided that I was obsessing about Ben because of Ben and not because of me. So I went up to his little house in the hills and told him how connected to him I still felt after all of these years. I admitted that the Ambien-fueled e-mail from Madrid didn't come from nowhere. And I asked for another chance.

"Is this because you're thirty-five and lonely?" Ben asked, a valid question that his friends would continue to insist was the answer.

I gave him a long speech about all of the experiences I had had in the last five years, about my moment on the beach in New Zealand where I realized I was ready to take someone along on my adventures. I was *different*. I had *grown* this year. I was *ready now*.

"You know I don't trust you, right?" Ben said.

"I know!"

"I'm dating people. I'm not just going to stop doing that," he continued.

"I get that."

"Last week my band played the Roxy and there were these Russian teenagers throwing glitter at me. I woke up in the morning with glitter in my beard. That was awesome."

"I know, I don't want you to stop having glitter in your beard," I promised.

He grilled me some more, and said he was really too busy with work for a relationship, and that my tits looked great in the Van Halen T-shirt I wore for precisely that reason. (Single girls: just go buy one. It's weird boy-bait. Don't know why, don't even like Van Halen, but trust me. If it helps mine is gray and V-necked.) I told him he didn't have to decide right then, to just think about it. But I had been running away from the truth for a long time—the simple fact that he moved me. That no matter what, he never left my heart. That I loved the way he looked at the world. He reached out, and pulled me to him.

We decided we shouldn't sleep together for a while, as a slow-it-down mechanism. So we started dating again, nervously, cautiously, and always stopping at third, and I tried to rebuild his trust while he held me at arm's length, and dated any extraordinarily young girl he wanted. We had said that we could each keep dating other people, but had to let the other know if things ever went past three or four dates with anyone. With so much ambivalence and distance, it was easy as pie for me to be *absolutely sure* this time . . . at least sure that I loved him. And so I wooed the shit out of him. Looking back on the e-mails now, you can practically hear me sweat. You can also imagine his quizzical look when you read his responses to my manic "*lovemetrustme*" tap dance. In one, he said that this new, unambivalent me seemed like a space alien to him, so different was she from who I had been for so many years.

"We're on the same page, we're just going at different speeds," Ben would say, after refusing to sleep with me, or go to my friends' gatherings, or tell any of his friends that we were dating again, or invite me to his gigs, or stop seeing other people. All of his behavior was totally fair given my sudden reappearance after so many years of rejection . . . but it was also incredibly unsettling. Ben was also a little different, and focused on work, and being in a band, and just sort of generally enjoying both kinds of booty that come with being a well-employed thirty-something man in Los Angeles who has the ability to get actresses work. But he was also different, I knew, because of me. Because I had sort of broken him. Which only made me want to fix him all the more. I wanted to clean up my mess.

A couple of months into this awkward and upsetting romantic situation, I got an invitation from Alex, the pretty Kiwi who had taken me into her house in Queenstown that previous autumn. She was going to Australia for the famous Byron Bay Bluesfest, and thought I should come along. I looked at my slow-moving, nonmonogamous heavy-petting relationship and wide-open employment schedule, and bought a plane ticket. Ben enthusiastically told me to have a great time on what he called my "passive-aggressive trip to Australia."

I firmly denied that it was passive-aggressive. It was just a great opportunity, and there was no reason not to go.

That being said, things were feeling very odd. I was ready to dive in, and Ben just wasn't.

He kept making it clear that I did not have a boyfriend. Within the previous couple of weeks we had discussed how I wasn't going on dates two or three with anyone, because I really just liked him.

"Huh," he replied, looking nervous.

"Which would be more anxiety-producing news for you right now: that I don't want to see other people, or that I fell madly in love with someone else?" I asked.

He laughed. "It's a tie."

So I wasn't sure what I was supposed to do in Australia. Shouldn't I be so true-blue in love that I shouldn't even want the freedom to enjoy the joys of an international romantic adventure? We had a long, unclear conversation about our status on his bedroom floor (where for some reason we always had long conversations) and then exchanged these nebulous e-mails:

FROM: KRISTIN
TO: BEN
RE: clarity

Just to reiterate what we discussed so I'm clear, what I think is happening is that you are not sleeping with other people right now, but like meeting/the possibility of hooking up with other people for the interest/freedom of it all. And this might not change in the next few months. Is that accurate?

FROM: BEN
TO: KRISTIN
RE: RE: clarity

I will always love the possibility of hooking up with 4,000 Russian teenagers. Right now I'm not sleeping with anyone. I like meeting new people, I'm not interested in random hookups. And, yes, this might not change by June. Time is so weird right now. June feels like a year from now and it feels like tomorrow.

Still stumped, I forwarded the (much longer) exchange to my girls from the Brisbane airport.

FWD: RE: RE: clarity

Do I have a boyfriend or not? When choosing your response, please take into account that I have already seen way more beautiful men in this Australian airport than I saw in all of New Zealand, and I'm going to have a lot of rage if I forgo them all and he is fucking Russian teenagers when I get home.

Sasha's response:

Let's try not to overanalyze. Have fun in Australia. If you end up on a koala rug with a kangaroo trainer, try not to post it on Facebook. I will be at Passover with your mother and am so so jealous.

My friend Parker's response:

How long is he going to punish and torture you? I say
go hook up with an Australian pirate and tell me all
about it. This could be your last chance! So jealous.

Alex had a Kiwi friend with a house in Byron Bay, a gorgeous little surf town where rainforest meets beach. Her friend was twenty-seven, and managed a popular nightclub in town, and Alex said his house was big and he was happy to have us. Those things were both true. What was also true was that he and his two roommates had thirteen other people staying with them for the festival.

"But don't worry," Alex promised cheerfully. "I've got a quiet little private space just for us!"

That space turned out to be one inflatable mattress on the floor of the bathroom, wedged in between the tub and the toilet. You entered the bathroom through the master bedroom, where the host's mother and stepfather were sleeping, and then through a walk-through closet, where another guy was sleeping. Six people were sleeping in the living room, and there were at least two in each of the two additional bedrooms. Three final people were in sleeping bags on the back porch. All of these people used our bathroom. We were piled in like stoned, juice-making refugees.

I tried to be as cheerful as Alex was when I suggested getting a hotel, but that's when she told me that she had a hundred dollars to her name *for the entire week*, and no credit cards, and wouldn't feel comfortable with me paying. Remember my travel rule about slumming it when your friends are in different financial situations than you are? Well, this was the trip where I really had to put my money where my mouth was, which happened to be in very close proximity to a toilet. (The town's hotels were also sold out. I might have checked.)

God bless Alex. Remember she was my savior in Queenstown, the kind of guardian angel who took me into her home and introduced me to extreme-sports guides. But, unfortunately, it turned out that Alex and I were as incompatible as travel partners as we had been perfect as roommates in her little house on the hill.

First incompatibility: my lack of patience with difficult eaters. Alex was an organic vegetarian who was allergic to onions. That pretty much excludes *all* vegetarian food. *Except*, apparently, Hare Krishna food. Did you even know there was such a thing as Hare Krishna food? Me neither! But, apparently, onions and garlic are outlawed in Hare Krishna cooking, since, as a random Hare Krishna website tells me, they "overstimulate the central nervous system, rooting the consciousness more firmly in the body"—i.e., they taste too good. Luckily, the little hippie town of Byron Bay had one such restaurant. So we ate there *every day*. Sometimes twice. This included when we were across town, doing something fun, in close proximity to delicious food that Alex would not eat. So we'd stop the fun, go across town, and get her food that was so bland it didn't alert your body to the fact that it was being fed.

Next travel-buddy problem: Alex's lack of desire to

compromise when it came to schedules. Every day, she slept next to our toilet until three in the afternoon, while I waited to go to the music festival, and watched the rain that never stopped falling. She then woke up, spent half an hour in the kitchen with a box of antioxidizing root vege-tables and the juicer, then spent hours primping, straight-ening her hair and putting on mascara. This was especially incredible because we were also about to put on gumboots and plastic trash bags to keep vaguely dry at a music fes-tival that was muddy in a hippies-are-pissing-everywhere, Woodstock sort of way. Watching someone straighten her hair before spending a night in a giant mud toilet during a rainstorm is a special kind of maddening, and might, per-haps, be a great way to torture me if you are trying to get state secrets out of me someday.

Because of Alex's lack of money, and her refusal to let me pay for anything, she needed to smuggle a flask of rotgut vodka into the festival in her bra for her drinking needs, which she would only drink mixed with fresh, or-ganic juices that always seemed to be sold on the opposite end of the enormous collection of stages and other *per-fectly fine juice stands*. She also wouldn't leave Byron Bay to go to another town where we could, say, sleep farther from where we shat. Because the housing in Byron Bay was free.

"Why don't you leave her?" Hope said, from Los An-geles, when I called her to complain, as Alex slept and the rain fell.

"I feel bad. We were supposed to have an adventure to-gether. I'm so mad you're not here. Also, I keep not kissing hot Australian surfers and I don't even know if I have a boyfriend," I complained.

"Everyone besides us sucks," Hope agreed. "Come home. I've decided I'm forgetting how to live with others, so I rented a room with these two hot thirtysomething professional dudes who surf. If your nonboyfriend boyfriend won't ever have sex with you, we're going to have the best summer ever in my new frat house."

"Promising!" I said, cheered.

And then I would e-mail Ben, who would reply to my updates about the trip, or the rain, or the koalas, but usually not my "I miss you"s.

I feel bad complaining about Alex, because she really is a lovely person. We just should never have been on this trip together. I wanted to see Australia, and Alex had lived in Australia and just wanted to see a few hours of music a night. We had different agendas. I tried to stay cheerful, because I thought we'd just be at the music festival a couple of days, and I was certainly living like a local, which I usually enjoyed. But a couple of days passed, and Alex wanted to stay longer. So we spent a full week in our little bathroom on our muddy mattress, and at night our host would do cocaine off our bathroom counter while those of us who had not stayed in bed until three in the afternoon tried to sleep.

But I didn't leave. And that was, really, for one reason. Everyone in the house was a good ten years younger than Alex and I were, and I could feel the pressure to *be cool with it,* to roll with it all the way I would have at twenty-three. One grim night in our host's club, Alex, who let's remember had spent the week making me trudge around town for organic, vegan, local food, asked if I wanted to accompany her and a man with stinky waist-long dreadlocks into the bathroom to snort some horse tranquilizers he had acquired from a veterinarian in Africa.

"They give them to livestock before surgery!" he said enticingly.

It was a low point for our collective travel mood, and I could see that Alex really wanted to reconnect via this shared equine narcotic experience, but I still declined for obvious reasons. And that made Alex really sad. I looked over at my dejected friend with her perfect hair, perched on a vinyl ottoman in a mirrored club lounge, sighed, and asked if this was going to, at long last, make her happy.

"So happy! I want to do this with you!" she said, her eyes pleading.

And so, much like the first time I tried Ecstasy a blue-haired man found on the ground in the name of saving another trip, I snorted my first and last bit of Special K off a credit card in a bathroom stall at age thirty-five to save this one. And then Alex and I danced, and then stared at a ceiling fan, and then did split leaps, and then sat on a curb with our heads in our hands, and then danced again, and then ran outside to sit on the curb again, just like best best friends. I can only assume that was because the horse tranquilizers were organic.

One day I finally snapped, and told Alex I was ready to see Australia, and I was going to force her to let me pay for it so we could do so. I got us a car, and we drove from Byron Bay into the rainforest, to hippie outpost Nimbin, where backpackers are brought by the busload to buy pot from Rainbow Park, a little grassy drug mall behind a pot "museum." We bought some pot cookies from a woman who assured us—not to worry—they were cooked over magic stones, we played pool with an ancient bearded madman who used to crochet bikinis for Harrods in the sixties, we got pictures of our auras taken at a crystal museum with a machine called an Auratron 2000.

I checked us in to a perfect little inn deep in the trees surrounded by deadly snakes, next to a river containing a deadly platypus. Everything in Australia, apparently, is deadly. Including, it turned out, Alex's attitude. The rain stopped falling the minute we left the beach and entered the rain forest, and Alex would sit in the room I was paying for and complain that we weren't still on the beach. We eventually made our way back to a different beach to appease that need, and I managed to get her to the late Crocodile Hunter's zoo to pet kangaroos and koalas by three p.m. one day. So, we both tried.

I had already planned on heading off on my own to spend a few days on a boat trip around the Whitsunday Islands, to see the Great Barrier Reef. So the time came to leave Alex, and we both pretended we hadn't been driving each other crazy, and hugged good-bye.

There are a lot of boats that cruise the Whitsundays, a chain of pretty little green-treed, white-sanded islands off the northeast coast of Australia. I chose my boat, the *Kiana*, carefully. The decision was price-based, but not because of money concerns. I knew that the cheapest boats would be filled with backpackers (college kids) and the most expensive boats would be filled with rich people (older couples). It's hard to find single thirtysomethings at all, but if you're going to find them anywhere, it's in the midpriced, slightly comfortable, but not super-fancy sphere. This is my best travel advice for solo grown-up travelers: shoot for the middle.

I showed up to the docks, and spotted my group of fourteen fellow sailors. They were perfect. Other than one fiftyish Irish nurse on holiday after a month volunteering in the Australian outback (whom I mentally celebrated for making me only the second oldest on the trip), they were all in their midtwenties to midthirties. There was only one couple among them. They were perfect, even though they were almost entirely German.

We all smiled at each other, and started to introduce ourselves. And that's when I met Dino.

Wearing only board shorts and flip-flops, Dino was very tall, very lean, and golden brown, with a smile that stretched across his face and possibly around the back of his head. With crazy, curly, sun-kissed hair styled similarly to Carrot Top's, Dino was the goofily cheerful kind of German.

Dino would later tell me that the moment we shook hands, he knew we were going to get together. It wouldn't happen for a couple of days, though. During those days, our boat collectively fell in love. We all sailed around in the perfect water, and snorkeled with five-foot-long turquoise fish who swam back and forth in front of us like dogs as we petted them. On one untouched white-sand beach, I wrote Ben's name in the sand and took a picture, to prove that I was thinking of him, wondering if he was thinking at all of me. There had been a cyclone in the ocean the week before, and so the water was cloudy, the perfect swimming-pool clarity ruined for our week. Things were no more clear above water, because through all of this, Dino and I circled each other.

One night, we stopped circling. It was after an afternoon and evening of beers and language exchange. (The Dutch taught us the word *swaffle*, which means "to hit something with your flaccid penis." This is apparently something the Dutch do often enough that they needed a word for it.) We were all sitting on the deck of the small boat, looking at the millions of stars in the hot night. And that's when Dino made the most hackneyed of all moves, the move that has been done so many times that I recently wrote it into an episode of *The Neighbors* in a scene where a teenaged boy had to make a ridiculous, obvious move that our teenaged girl would reject, because it was so ridiculous and obvious.

He reached around my shoulders to point out the constellations. As you know from seeing this move in movies, it positions the pointer's face right next to its intended target: the pointee's face. So, now cheek to cheek, Dino showed me the Southern Cross.

And, because I was on a boat, and he smelled like coconut sunscreen, and the move was hilarious, and I feared I was spinning my romantic wheels at home and could come home without a romantic story only to be rejected by a guy I suspected was dating me out of morbid curiosity . . . it worked.

We kissed for about four hours on the deck of that tiny boat, first in front of everyone, then, after everyone went down to our communal sleeping area, just in front of the captain. It was very PG and very, very hot. Like if Olivier Martinez from *Unfaithful* was starring in *High School Musical.*

We spent the next two days as the ship's couple. Snuggling, kissing underwater, buddying up on dives. Dino turned out to be a former rapper, and rapped for me in German, which was the only thing more hilarious and ridiculous than his Southern Cross move. I vacillated between feeling guilt about Ben and confidence that this was the only logical way to protect myself. *Of course* I wouldn't be doing this if Ben had taken me back with open arms. *Yes*, I wanted things to work out with Ben. But . . . what if they didn't?

Ben had been right. I *had* taken a passive-aggressive trip to Australia, just like, really, I had taken a passive-aggressive trip to New Zealand the year before. That trip had been to prove to everyone and to myself that I was *not* the kind of girl who cried at home after a work failure. And I was also *not* the kind of girl who waited for a man who couldn't promise that he would let her back into his life. But what that meant was that I *was* apparently the kind of girl who goes back to someone she rejected, says she loves him and wants him and is ready for a relationship . . . and then kisses a German on a boat.

Ultimately, this trip was me proving to myself that I hadn't lost myself. But let's be honest: if you don't ever lose yourself, it means you're not entirely in the game.

After four days, the boat pulled back into harbor. Dino and I had one night in town together before we were flying off in different directions. We got a hotel room, and showered, and changed. And that's when I saw Dino in clothes for the first time, after a week of only swimsuits.

Oy. So European.

Tight, sleeveless red T-shirt. Way overproduced jeans, seams and bleach splashes and extra pockets everywhere. So much hair gel. So much cologne. And, on top of it all, a white trucker cap spray-painted with multicolored fluorescent graffiti.

"Ooh! Look at you!" I said.

It's funny how you can tell so much more about a person dressed than you can naked. If I had met Dino on land, in clothes, we never would have gotten together. It's so easy to fall for someone when you're floating in the middle of an ocean, metaphorically or actually. Back at home, or even back on land, all of the little things that keep you from falling in love a thousand times a day when you aren't on vacation come flooding in, and ruin it.

10

"Even Björk Is Having Babies"

Los Angeles International → Reykjavík Keflavík
Departing: July 18, 2009

The only thing sadder than finding yourself on a trip with a terrible traveling companion is finding yourself on a trip with a perfect one. And that is because they never last.

Sasha had been my best travel buddy in my twenties, but then she met her husband and spent several years getting knocked up, and I lost her. I had gotten her back for a few days in 2009 for a trip to Hawaii, our first girls' trip in the six years since she'd started her family. And she cut loose by not having a single drink the entire trip. She didn't like the way alcohol made her feel anymore. We woke up early, and played in the sun, and went to bed with books after an early dinner. And her one-piece mommy swimsuit kept her crooked Russian barbed-wire infinity tramp stamp hidden the whole time.

Parker was Sasha's replacement when she started breeding. We met through a mutual friend when she moved to Los Angeles after a year in Hong Kong with a long-term boyfriend. We were twenty-nine, and both single for the first time in our adult lives. One night at the end of their time in Hong Kong, Parker's boyfriend had proposed, and, just like in a romantic comedy, the word *No* had popped out of her mouth despite the fact that for years she had been sure it was going to be *Yes*. Fun, adorable, newly single and game for anything, she had been a real find for me. But I messed up: I met an adorable, smart guy, who was friends with my then boyfriend, and I introduced him to Parker. A couple of years later, my ex and I were throwing them an engagement party.

Parker did not, ideally, want to meet her future husband when she did. She was only about a year out of her six-year relationship, and she and I were both gearing up for our first swing at single-girl-land. Parker's realization that she had met the love of her life was a bittersweet one: she was glad she found this great guy, but she *really* wished she had done so a year or two later.

Maybe as a result of this, Parker did a much better job of staying fun than many of my other hitched friends did. She accompanied Emma and me to Greece, where she happily tossed plates onto the floors of bars shouting "OPRAH!" all night long. Her husband still complains about the monthlong "Vegas flu" Parker brought home from a Halloween girls' weekend in Las Vegas, where we danced the night away dressed as two members of a very sluttily garbed Girl Scout troop. At around five in the morning, Parker had a love affair with a lollipop that was so intense she felt the need to share said lollipop with the mouths of half of the club. Don't ever do that. The World Health Organization almost had to be called in.

So when I invited Parker to join me on a trip to Iceland, she happily left her nice husband behind for a week of throwback single-girl travel adventures. But this time when Parker packed her girl-trip bag, it was not filled with slutty versions of children's uniforms, or Grecian beachwear. This time it was filled with fertility drugs, thermometers, and pee sticks.

Parker was trying to get pregnant. She woke up every morning of the trip to take her temperature, write down the results, and take her pills. She had been at all of this for a year, too, so my normally easygoing friend was on edge—still a great time, but irritable, concerned (understandably) about the hot springs and copious amounts of vodka involved in a trip to Iceland. But the year of chasing babies had also made her feel heavy, and old, and she needed this vacation.

I was on edge, too. I was six months into my second round of dating Ben, and he was not coming around. He had finally started sleeping with me, but was not diving in emotionally.

"He wants to be in control," Hope said. "You popped back into his life and he wants to control how he reacts to it."

"I'm afraid of being a goner," was how Ben put it.

Work, or the lack thereof, was not helping me be patient with Ben, either. The comedy business had slowed way down, and I was not working on a show that year as a result. I was writing a pilot for Warner Bros. (about a group of terminally single friends with broken romantic pickers who decide to just give up and "marry" each other—where do I come up with this stuff???), but that required very few hours per day. Meanwhile, Ben was in a crazy work mode, so time was passing in a much different way for him. I was laying myself out there, and full of time and energy to give to him, and he wasn't. And I was starting to think he was never going to.

"He's different," Parker said. "You might have broken him."

"He knows that as soon as you really get him you'll come up with a reason for it not to work," Sasha said.

Ouch. So I went to Iceland.

Iceland is maybe the weirdest place in all the world. If you're like most people, what you know about Iceland adds up to one word: *Björk*. There was no one in the U.S. who did not respond to the news that we were going to Iceland with the sentence "Cool, you gonna see Björk?"

Little does the entire world know that there is so much more to see! For starters, there are all of the fairies, gnomes, ghosts, and trolls. Now, that might sound like I am being just as ignorant as the people who think that everyone who goes to Iceland sees Björk, but if you go to a tourism office in Iceland, you will see that on their official tourist map, in addition to the drawings delineating the locations of whales, puffins, and waterfalls, there are drawings of fairies, gnomes, ghosts, and trolls. If you're like us, you will wonder, "I wonder what this ghost drawing represents!" and then you will look at the map's legend, which will tell you that what the ghost drawing represents is a ghost.

Icelanders love to tell you that it's a stereotype that they all believe in otherworldly creatures. And then you read about the Iceland Road Authority bringing in a medium to ask the elves who reside in a pile of rocks that lie in the path of a proposed road if the *elves* would mind if the rocks were moved. When this happened near a town called Hafnarfjörður (not misspelled), the medium said that the elves unfortunately did not want their home relocated. Since plenty of "suspicious and unexplainable phenomena" had been occurring near the job site, the Road Authority *listened to the elves and rerouted their road.*

"Our basic approach is not to deny this phenomenon. There are people who can negotiate with the elves, and we make use of that," the *state-employed* engineer told Reuters.

One night on the Snæfellsnes Peninsula (Parker and I just called it Snuffleupagus), I noticed on our map that there was a ghost icon in the hills behind our hotel. I went up to the front desk, and asked Björn (real name), the handlebar-mustachioed desk guy, if ghosts really lived in those mountains.

"Oh, no," he said, scoffing. "Ghosts live everywhere."

So, they're weird. But there's just no reasonable way they couldn't be. What if you were one of like ten people living on an island in the North Atlantic that is dark half of the year? Ever since a couple of boats of Vikings made their way to this frigid island carrying the prettiest women they could rape and pillage along the way, Icelanders have been getting weird to get through the winter. And they've done well. It's clear their ancestors raped only the best. (And have you seen *Thor*? Maybe they didn't so much have to rape. "Oooh, Thor! No! Please don't take me by force from my toothless Welsh farm husband! No, really, don't throw me over your big, bare shoulder!") Those first Icelanders were so good-looking, to this day Iceland proudly claims to have the most beautiful women in the world, a claim supported by this tiny country's unusual number of Miss World winners.

This flies in the face of my theory that the best-looking people are always in countries with large, diverse, mixed-up genetic pools. (Versus, say, New Zealand, where too many Brits bred with each other for too long on a small island. Big teeth, no chins, real mess.) But in Iceland, the good taste of the Vikings has caused a small gene pool to turn out great! That isn't to say that Icelanders are backward, and think mixing too closely with your relatives is okay. In fact, to keep that from happening, an enterprising Icelander recently invented the "Accidental Incest" app. In a country of 320,000 people, the odds of accidentally kissing your cousin are far higher than you might like. So with this app, you and the hot Viking at the bar just bump phones, and it tells you if you are related. "Bump the app before you bump in bed" is the catchy slogan. Really.

All of those semi-related, tall, white, blond people went *nuts* for my tiny, gorgeous, Peruvian friend, Parker. We would go to pay for our dinner in restaurants only to find that the bill had been anonymously paid by a "gentleman admirer" who had enjoyed watching Parker eat cod. We got pulled over for speeding, and the Chippendales-looking Icelandic cop asked Parker where her family was from, complimented her skin, let us out of the ticket, and led us to our destination, a nearby farmer's hot springs. After years of traveling with her tall, white husband, who was always the exotic person of interest in countries where the people were smaller or darker, Parker had a great time. Her sad little unimpregnated heart grew five sizes that trip.

One of the many Icelanders who fell for Parker was a Viking masseur. It was during one of the top five travel experiences of my life: a floating massage at the Blue Lagoon.

The Blue Lagoon is Iceland's biggest tourist attraction; annually it attracts more people than live in Iceland. Almost twice as many. It turns out that a glacial-blue, milky hot spring in the middle of an isolated black lava field is Valhalla. Surrounding the huge, steamy, mint-colored pool is creamy, soft white mud that bathers slather all over their faces before wading up to a wooden dock in the middle of the pool for drinks. Even in July, when the days are twenty hours long, it doesn't get much warmer than fifty degrees, so your beer stays perfectly cold as you swim around in the warm water in your face mask. We had booked "floating massages," not really knowing what they were, but we were told to head over to a semiprivate corner of the lagoon to get them.

Two Vikings in swimsuits met us, and waved us onto thin, floating mattresses. Thor (actual name) and Dante (same) then took fleece blankets, soaked them in the womb-temperature water, and covered our bodies with them, so we wouldn't be even the least bit chilly on our exposed side.

The only way to massage a floating person is to kind of wrap your arms around them, and pull them close, using all of your body to hold them still as you rub them. So for the next hour and a half, Parker and I were embraced and rubbed by these near-naked descendants of the first Thor, with sun and cool wind on our faces, and warm water and big hands everywhere else. The experience was like having the best sex ever while in the womb. When it was over, my masseur/favorite person in my life whispered, "Now just relax," and gave me a little push. I drifted away, into a quiet alcove, and after a few minutes of floating in the breeze, I felt Parker bob up next to me.

Finally opening my eyes, I looked over at my equally blissed-out friend.

"I kinda feel like you just cheated on your husband," I said.

"I was thinking the exact same thing," she replied.

By the way, my little Peruvian friend's masseur insisted he could only massage her properly if she let him untie her bikini top. The white girl's masseur seemed to be able to rub her just fine with her top on.

"Are you Indian?" Parker's masseur asked her as we emerged from the water. "Your skin is so beautiful."

Iceland is possibly the most stunning country in the world. We rode tiny, fuzzy Icelandic horses across emerald green, spongy tundra, we snowmobiled across glaciers under blue skies, we strolled around gardens filled with tiny painted houses (for the fairies who live in gardens), we drank rum-on-the-two-thousand-year-old-rocks with a boat driver who chipped us off a piece of ancient glacial ice as we cruised by. We rented a car to get around, and so spent a lot of the time on nearly empty roads just driving.

As we drove, Parker and I talked a lot about timing. We had both been girls and women who were very good at setting goals, going after them, and making them happen. Her inability to get pregnant when she wanted was flying in the face of that. Her husband had come along sooner than she hoped, so she hadn't gotten to choose how long she got to be single, either. I had tried to push pause on my relationship with Ben (and settling down in general), and then restart it when the time was right for me. But Ben's life hadn't paused. He had moved on, and the love I went back for was no longer there in the same way. The connection was, but the time had passed for his heart to be really available. Maybe he was too different, or maybe the effects of time and history had made me less attractive to him. But things had kept moving.

Furthermore, the world hadn't paused. The good ones *had* been snatched up, just like people always said they would be. I had always scoffed at this, because I knew so many fantastic guys who were single into their thirties and forties. But chasing some of those fantastic guys unsuccessfully for years had shown me what everyone was talking about when they said "the good ones." They meant the ones who want to commit, who are excited to build a family and life with a *grown-up*. Those *do* disappear. I didn't regret my path of fun and freedom for a moment, and really didn't wish I had settled down earlier, but there was going to be a cost.

My friends who met their spouses young have often told me they live vicariously through my adventures. That they sometimes think about the oats they never got a chance to sow. There is a trade-off for both their choice and mine. I used to beat my head over Vito, when he was struggling for years over how he wanted to be with me, but also wanted a life that wasn't compatible with my life. He couldn't believe that he couldn't have everything, and so just wouldn't choose. And I would tell him, so full of twentysomething wisdom, that life is almost never about choosing between one thing you really want and another thing you don't want at all. If you're lucky, and healthy, and live in a country where you have enough to eat and no fear that you're going to get shot when you walk out your door, life is an endless series of choosing between two things you want *almost equally*. And you have to evaluate and determine which awesome thing you want infinitesimally more, and then give up that other awesome thing you want *almost exactly as much*. You have to trade awesome for awesome.

Everyone I knew, no matter what they chose, was at least *a little* in mourning for that other thing.

Parker and I were standing in line at the airport at the end of our Icelandic adventure when Parker gasped, got a huge smile on her face, and pointed. I followed her finger, and there was a brunette woman in a short, polka-dotted baby-doll dress and striped knee socks. She was holding the hand of a little girl who was wearing only a shirt and panties, and was absolutely too old to be going without pants. But this was a little girl who never really had a shot at dressing appropriately, because this little girl's mommy was Björk. We *had* gone to Iceland and seen Björk.

Some things are inevitable. There are repercussions to your actions, logical cause-and-effects, like if you go to Iceland you will see Björk. Like if you are Björk's child, you will go pantsless in public far longer than is appropriate. Like if you break someone's heart, and leave them to go find yourself on years of solo adventures, they will be different and unavailable when you come back.

Parker got pregnant with her first daughter a few weeks after we got home. She swears it's because she got the flu, and had to just give in and lie down for a week instead of working twelve-hour days. She got pregnant with her second daughter two years later, and Iceland was our last "single-girl" trip together. Yet another travel partner had bitten the dust, and I was still on the road.

11

"The Land of Milk and Funny"

By this point in my life, I was very used to getting the following call from my agent when springtime, and hence TV staffing season for writers, rolled around:

"Got you a meeting on this show about single people. Go in there and tell your terminally-single-whorey stories."

Sometimes, if the job interviewer was a more reserved type, he might also add the following:

"Don't Kristin Newman all over the place."

Then he would hang up, and I would go into the meeting, trying to be not-too-Kristin-but-just-Kristin-enough, and tell my crazy stories, all in the hopes that the interviewer would see an endless vessel of episode ideas in the wealth of neuroses and life experiences before them, since that's how a sitcom writer gets a job.

During the staffing season that accompanied my thirty-seventh year, that meeting turned especially meta, since one of the executives for whom I was to trot out my terminally single stories was a woman who was one week away from marrying my ex-boyfriend Matt. I decided to just own it, and chirped to the nice woman as I left, "My latest funny terminally single story is now having to tell my funny terminally single stories to my ex-boyfriend's fiancée!" She laughed, kindly, and hugged me good-bye. Like you can do when you're healthy and have won.

Another upsetting trend was suddenly happening in my work life: people kept pitching me books to turn into shows with deeply upsetting messages. Worse, the pitches for these grim titles would always start with a speech like, "Kristin, I have this book that's *perfect* for you. It's called *My Formerly Hot Life*."

About a woman who used to be hot, and is now forty.

Or *The Panic Years*.

About women "on the wrong side of *twenty-five* without a ring."

This book was pitched to me by a good friend, a producer who also happens to be a forty-five-year-old, happily single man.

"What about my life choices would ever make you think I would want to put a message like this out in the world? *Twenty-five? Wrong side?*" I demanded.

"Oh, right," he said, thinking I was insane.

It made me more determined than ever to break the stereotype: I would *not* be a sad, bitter Bridget Jones, waiting for her prince/barrister. I would not panic about my age. I would enjoy my life if it killed me.

A couple of weeks after I came home from Iceland, Ben and I broke up. He wasn't as in it as he needed to be, and we both knew it. His "I love you"s this time were reticent, usually sandwiched between a "sure" and a "but"—*Sure, I love you, but* . . . There was a deep sadness about walking away, but also a bit of relief—I had gone back, and tried to fix my mess, but it was unfixable. At least it wasn't hanging out there, a question that needed to be answered, a big love that I had passed by. We would say later that the first time around it was my turn to be the narcissist, and the second time around it was his. So we were even, which hurt, but felt correct.

The night we broke up, I had a dream. I was in Antarctica, and I felt I had never seen something so wonderful. In the dream, I had mistakenly gone to Antarctica in the winter, and so it was unexpectedly dark. But it was much, much more beautiful than I had pictured it would look in the sun. There were very kind people there, and magical lights, and cathedral-like, glowing cliffs of translucent, turquoise ice, and I was shocked that this place that was so dark and cold and unexpected could be the most spectacular place I had ever been. I took the dream as a good sign that I was heading to something really transcendent and surprising by making the hard choice to leave Ben. Walking away from the compromise that being with him represented was going to lead to me finding something really spectacular.

And wouldn't you know, about three months after Ben and I broke up, Father Juan came to America.

Juan and I had stayed sporadically in touch, and I had noticed on Facebook that he was planning a trip to New York. I immediately pointed out that Los Angeles was on the very same continent, and he quickly agreed it seemed silly to come so far and not see California.

He would be in town for Thanksgiving, and so he would also be meeting my family. My family on Thanksgiving also includes Sasha's family, since there have been many Thanksgivings when Sasha, whom my mother calls her "soul daughter," would host my family while I was off gallivanting. Sasha is a much better daughter to my mother in a couple of departments, holiday-throwing and grandchild-bearing being the big ones. Sasha's first child got a gift from my mother of a baby-size leather jacket my mother had bought several years earlier for her "grandma hope chest." I took too long, though, so the jacket went to Sasha.

I had no idea what was going to happen when Juan came to visit. I didn't even know if he was visiting as a friend or as something more. Let's remember that he had never slept with me, and the last time I'd seen him in Argentina it had been platonic. Five years had passed since our first romantic time in Buenos Aires. To cover all my bases, I waxed everything I had and put clean sheets on the guest bed.

I picked Juan up from the airport, and, not at all shockingly, he looked glorious after that fifteen-hour flight. I nervously took the exhausted man sight-seeing: we went out for a walk on the Venice boardwalk. We got cheap Thai massages, and went for his first tacos with some friends. I was keeping him moving. We were shy with each other, small-talking and keeping our distance. I started to worry: maybe this *was* just a platonic visit to see L.A. But after dinner, we went back to my house, where we had put his bag in the guest room.

"You know, there is one problem with that room," I said as we lingered awkwardly in the kitchen, getting glasses of water. "There aren't curtains on the window, so the sun comes in *really* bright in the morning. Might be *too* bright for you up there."

He smiled at me, and took my face in his hands, and I took him to my room. And that almost-priest had brought a condom all the way from South America this time.

The rest of that week was a rush of giddy joy. Thanksgiving with my family was sweet and delightful. Sasha's timid, soft-spoken stepmother pulled me aside to gush:

"Kristin, he's *so handsome.* It's like there's some kind of *light* coming out of him."

My mother was worried. She had been worried since I first came home from Argentina five years earlier enamored with Juan, and she was more worried now as she watched me fluttering around. She thought Juan was as lovely as everyone did, but I think she saw in my eyes exactly what had been in her eyes twenty years earlier, when her Latin lover, Laszlo, went back to Latin America, her heart in his hand, the rest of her left behind in the fetal position in California.

As a result of her heartbreak, she had tried hard to keep me from following my genetically predisposed need for international adventure down the same road hers had led her. When I was sixteen, not long after Laszlo left, my mother and I sat through our twenty-third viewing of *Dirty Dancing*. At the end of what was, and maybe still is, my all-time-favorite losing-it scene in American cinema, when a still-large-nosed Jennifer Grey asks a shirtless Patrick Swayze to "dance with her," which boy oh boy does he ever do and how, I turned to my wildly depressed, afghan-wrapped mother and said, "Well, it doesn't get any better than that." She then gave me advice that I'm sure she hoped would save me years of heartache looking for what she had just lost:

"Kristin, it doesn't get that good."

After Thanksgiving, I took Juan up to Santa Barbara wine country, where we rented a house for the weekend with three other couples. A newly pregnant Parker and her husband were there, as were Hope and her new boyfriend (finally!) and another constantly single comedy writer friend, Erin, and her boyfriend (finally!). It was a weekend of wine and friendship and love, and I was *one of the couples for once* (finally!). Juan and I made up for our five sex-free years, and we all cooked and drank and visited miniature horses and danced in empty saloons. It was a golden weekend, and I was deliriously, deliriously happy.

The week came to an end, and Juan didn't try to change his flight to stay longer, and he didn't ask me when we were going to see each other again. He just kissed me sweetly, said the week had been amazing . . . and left.

And man I was blue. Feeling singler than single, and lying around the house too much. I still wasn't working since I hadn't gotten staffed on a show, and the pilot I wrote that year was not getting shot. (The networks buy hundreds of scripts every year, make a dozen or two, and put a handful on the air. It's incredibly upsetting to be a writer of one of these hundreds of unmade scripts unless you set out knowing you're getting paid to write a script that will never get made, and then you can just crank out one a year in peace, grateful that you've covered your mortgage. It's a nonsensical process, and business, and life.)

So I was lying around my house too much. My mom called me one day, and I braced myself for some sentiment that would make me feel worse. But instead, the woman who normally cautioned me against running away so much suggested something amazing:

"Pistol, it sounds like you need a trip."

It made me cry, how known and accepted this advice from this particular person made me feel.

I decided to go to Israel. I had an idea for a script that would be set there, so research was in order. The idea was to write a drama, something edgy for cable, about expats living in Jerusalem, living regular lives in the middle of the conflict. The comedy television scene had slowed down almost to a crawl, and it was time to broaden my writing horizons.

Of course, I wasn't Jewish and knew next to nothing about the Israeli political situation. I bought really embarrassing books, like *Teach Yourself: The Middle East Peace Crisis!* and *The Israeli/Palestinian Conflict for Dummies!* I read them quickly, absolutely unwilling to take any of these books on a plane with actual Middle Easterners. As I started to fall in love with a new country, and spend my day thinking about something new, my mood lifted.

I got my intrepid single-girl traveler buddy, Astrid, who's traveled alone even more extensively than I have, and we went to the Holy Land. Getting there was not simple, however. First two single girls had to get through security.

When you fly to Israel with El Al, there is a multi-tiered, one-on-one interview process where you are given a security rating, from one to seven. A one is for a Jewish Israeli, and gets the fewest security delays. A seven is for a probable terrorist.

It turns out that single Western women "of a certain age" are much closer to a seven than a one. Apparently there have been incidents where sad, middle-aged single girls get involved in online relationships with "handsome Israelis" who then invite these lonely hearts to come visit them in Israel. "Just pick up a package and bring it for me, and then our hearts will be forever joined Old Testament–style," these men promise. Then the sad, lonely girl picks up the package, having no idea that her "boyfriend" is actually an Arab terrorist, and unknowingly tries to bring her lover's bomb on a plane.

Basically, single women in their thirties are a national security threat to the state of Israel.

Combine our dangerous marital status with the fact that my tiny blond friend Astrid liked to do things like travel alone to Tunisia, and you have two hours of security checks. They stripped us of everything but our passports, and we were handed the rest of our things on the plane.

Except we didn't get everything back. In the search process, they apparently forgot to replace an entire bag of my clothes. So I got to Israel without anything to cover the top half of my body. Since Astrid had forgotten her contact lenses, we said we were the blind leading the topless.

Before we left the States, I wrote the following six words on my Facebook page:

"Anyone know anyone interesting in Israel?"

Two things happened: every Jewish man I knew responded with the words "I love Israel! I got my first hand job on the beach in Israel!" Apparently, those Birthright teen trips to Israel have been both wildly successful in bringing young Jews together and wildly unsuccessful in that hundreds of millions of wasted little Jews have been spilled upon those chosen sands. The second thing that resulted from my Facebook post was that I got introduced to about a hundred incredible people. Let me tell you, a couple of people in Hollywood know a couple of people in Israel.

It was remarkable who we met. Secular kibbutzniks, converted Hasidic Americans, Israeli comedy writers, gay pro-Palestinian European diplomats (and their new test-tube baby freshly grown in a woman in India), American-Israeli Harvard MBA fighter pilot finance guys, Palestinian shopkeepers, sons of Bedouin chiefs, divorced Christian Arab-Israelis, television network presidents, Nobel Peace Prize laureates. I'm not sure if we met the most interesting people in Israel, or if Israel is just a country exclusively full of the kind of people about whom Spielberg could make a movie. But the array of stories I heard and experiences I had in that country were unlike any trip I've ever taken, before or since.

Our first night in Tel Aviv, Astrid and I met up with a group of Israeli comedy writers. They had worked together on *Eretz Nehederet* (A Wonderful Land), which is Israel's version of *Saturday Night Live*. Over drinks with these five writers, I asked them a million questions about life and culture and the political situation there. And that's when I started to learn that "Depends who you ask" is always the first part of every answer to every question you ask anyone in Israel.

The writers talked about Judaism and therapy and annoying network script notes, and told Holocaust and dick jokes and complained about their wives. It was exactly like a day at the office in L.A. The group even had the same gender breakdown as a Hollywood writers' room: it was four schlubby thirtyish men, and one blond woman, who also happened to be the granddaughter of former Israeli prime minister Shimon Peres.

"Is this usually how the comedy rooms look? A bunch of guys and you?" I asked her.

She smiled that same smile I see on every female comedy writer's face in L.A., and she shrugged and nodded just like we do.

———

Astrid had a boyfriend back in L.A. They had been together about a year and a half, and he was a very handsome, impeccably dressed, self-described "dandy." He was also an underemployed "producer" who had told her at the outset of the relationship that he was not looking for anything serious. She didn't believe him, and so was now saying "I love you" to a man who wouldn't say it back because he was afraid of making women mad at him when he didn't follow through on promises. "I love you" was a promise he wasn't willing to make.

He was exhausting in lots of other ways, too. We had all gone to Mammoth to ski and snowboard earlier in the year, and Astrid, an expert skier who normally hit the slopes as the lifts opened, spent half the day tagging after her boyfriend as he fussed with several sets of rented equipment, constantly dissatisfied and trading things in, wanting a new jacket, different boots, sassier goggles . . . She finally snapped when the man who had gone skiing hundreds of times took his ski ticket and the wire wicket you use to attach it to your jacket, and held them out to her like a child, pouting:

"Will you do it?"

Even though they were polar opposites, she loved him, and Skyped from Israel with the man who *kept telling her* he was nowhere near even wanting to move in together, let alone get married or have kids, like she was ready to do. *Which was what he had been telling her for almost two years.* She vacillated between making excuses for him, declaring she was ready to end it, and, way too often, calling herself "unlovable." Astrid was a lawyer, and an über-tough broad for a tiny ex-gymnast, so all of this always came in the form of "jokes," but it was wearing on her. She was thirty-five, beautiful, smart, well-traveled, successful, and acutely aware that her romantic history comprised a long list of less-than-worthy men who had all eventually left.

Getting on a plane was her medicine, too.

Astrid and I rented a car and started driving through the desert, past camels and Bedouin encampments, through the West Bank and the "illegal" settlements. (Not everyone calls them "illegal," obviously. There are a million things in Israel that have two or more politically charged names, like the "Security" wall that is also called the "Separation" wall. *Depends who you ask.*) We put on lip gloss before we got to every military checkpoint, which were all packed with young, fit, tanned soldiers. Man, does olive green look great with a Sephardic complexion. We took pictures of every highway exit sign, in awe at the places we were passing: Bethlehem! Nazareth! Sodom! *and* Gomorrah! Places so merged with myth that they had to be mythical, and yet there they were, filled with life and liquor stores, churches and mosques and temples and sewers. There are still sheep in THE "shepherd's field," but there is also a "Stars and Bucks" Palestinian Starbucks rip-off across the street. There is a tattoo parlor next to the Church of the Nativity, which houses THE manger.

We went to the Dead Sea, which is *way* more fun than you think it's going to be, and also way uglier. The floating is so great I actually fell asleep for a twenty-minute nap while lying on my back in that viscous water. But the aesthetics of the Dead Sea are kind of a drag. It turns out that the region is sort of a tiny Vegas for Russians with skin conditions, since the Russian health care system apparently pays for them to come soak in the healing waters for weeks at a time. Most of the hotel employees of the ugly high-rises around the Dead Sea don't even speak Hebrew or English, just Russian, because there is such a parade of large, white, eczema-ridden Eastern Bloc tourists. They cover their generally large bodies in black mud, and bake in the hundred-degree sun next to the saltiest sea on earth, usually smoking cigarettes. Remember the scene at Posto Nove in Brazil? The Dead Sea is the polar opposite of Posto Nove.

After beach day with the itchy Russians, we drove all the way to the bottom of Israel, where we had some of the best snorkeling of my life in the clear turquoise sea that is oddly called Red, and met up for a couple of hours on the sand with Avi, the blue-eyed Israeli I met years before in Patagonia. Since I had last seen him he had been all over the world, even living in New York City for a year selling Ahava Dead Sea products at one of those carts in the malls that are always manned by aggressive Israeli salesmen asking if you want to try some lotion. We all swam with the rainbow-hewed fish in the azure water, and then he gave us a ride to the border, waving good-bye while we walked through the razor-wired no-man's-land to Jordan.

Eilat, Israel → Wadi Musa, Jordan

We would spend three days in Jordan, because we wanted to see Petra. You know Petra, it's the pink stone ruins in *Indiana Jones and the Last Crusade.* They've been called half as old as time, and we joked that we were a quarter.

We walked and rode horses and finally camels through miles of hot, pink stone canyon walls that were somehow carved into the columned, ornately decorated facade of a glorious ancient city. Bedouins—nomadic, desert-dwelling tribesmen—still live in some of the caves in Petra, and many more of them have opened cafés and shops, or offer camel, donkey, and horse rides. At the end of the road, we stopped for a cold tea and met some Bedouin guys in a small café inside a cave in front of one of the temples. There was one extremely sexy man in black eyeliner who wore all white and lay on a carpet talking on his cell phone. He turned out to be a son of a Bedouin chief, and his father had eighteen kids and two wives. Sexy dude was number sixteen or seventeen from wife number two.

We chatted with him and his friends, who all wanted to make sure we understood that the Bedouins were the *last free men.* They could lie where they liked and move when they wanted, freed from "homes" and "possessions" to *just be men.*

"So, where did you sleep last night?" I asked the chief's son.

He pointed with his cell phone over a hill, where there was a small town of concrete houses, with satellite dishes on top. "My mom's house."

These last free men with satellite dishes had lots of stories they wanted to tell. Like one about their cousin, who is now living with an Italian woman he met when she was here visiting Petra, *just like us*. When their cousin and the Italian woman met he was eighteen and she was fifty, and now they are married, and living in her house in Italy.

"It was just true love," the teenager's cousins all told us, with straight faces.

"Okay, so if we're still single at fifty, we'll just come back here and get one too," Astrid said to me.

The Bedouin boys did not like our dismissive jokes about true love. They wanted to know if we had seen the book that is for sale in many, many cave shops in Petra. It's called *I Married a Bedouin*, and is a memoir by a Kiwi nurse who came to Petra in the seventies, met a hot Bedouin boy in black eyeliner, converted to Islam, bore him many sons as one of many wives, and never left. It is *very, very* important to the men of Petra that you know this story.

"Why not sleep under the stars tonight with us?" they suggested. "We will make you a real Bedouin meal, and sleep in the nature way. And if we are feeling the feeling, then we will do that, if not, we will only sleep."

While pretty tempting to sleep in the nature way with the steamy young man in white, especially once we learned that camel's milk is also known in these parts as "Bedouin Viagra," it ultimately seemed like a bad idea. (Fine, I would have done it. But Astrid had a headache and even I was not going to head into the desert for the night alone with a tribe of camel's-milk-fueled Bedouins.) We did manage to convince our Bedouin prince to hike up his skirt and help us climb way up the rocks alongside the three-story temple for a normally off-limits walk on top of the dome that was supposed to be Bedouin-only. The hot desert wind felt great, and the view of it blowing around the prince's skirts as he walked on top of the dome was stupendous.

It was almost good enough to make you feel the feeling.

Wadi Musa, Jordan → Jerusalem, Israel

I am not a religious person, but I believe Jerusalem is the most important place on the planet. You don't have to be a believer to be moved when you stand on that ground, every single stone bled over, and watch people from three major religions and every country in the world file in by the busload every minute of every day to the place they believe was chosen by God. The city buzzes with the energy that is poured into it. I had about a hundred conversations with a variety of people about who should lay claim to Jerusalem, but my time in the city made me absolutely certain of what I think: Jerusalem belongs to the world. Not to the Israelis, not to the Palestinians. Just as the Vatican is not a part of Italy, that place should not be part of any state.

And . . . commence death threats.

Anyway, I had one of the most interesting twenty-four hours of my life in Jerusalem. Here was the plan: Sasha had an Israeli tour-guide cousin named Omri who was going to take us on a tour of the city. Omri was a worldly, secular child of Holocaust orphans who had met on a kibbutz as teenagers, after the war. He spent half of his year taking Israelis on tours around the world, and the other half taking foreigners around Israel. He also believed in a two-state solution to the Israeli-Palestinian crisis. So it was with that perspective that we would get the history of Jerusalem. After a day with him, we would go to a Friday Shabbat dinner with a Hasidic Orthodox family who were related to a Californian friend, and who lived in the Jewish Quarter in the Old City. Then on Saturday, when the entire city is closed down for the Sabbath, we would join my childhood friend and his Argentine-diplomat boyfriend for brunch with some gay and lesbian European diplomats who worked for their countries on Palestinian humanitarian-aid projects.

So, basically, we were spending twenty-four hours hearing just about every perspective. *Depends who you ask*, right? And so we asked everyone. The best part, though, is that they all answered. Israel and I were a real match, conversationally speaking. Israelis have no patience for niceties or bullshit or small talk. They love direct questions and will always give you direct answers. They thrive on the probing and the personal, and delight in finding ways to laugh at things that are heavy and dark. Which is my specialty. You'll never find better conversation than you'll find in Israel. It made me want to move there.

Omri started our day by taking us to the top of the Mount of Olives for a view of the entire Old City. The Mount is covered in groups of singing Christians as well as thousands of graves, because it abuts the gate through which the Messiah is supposed to walk when he returns (or shows up for the first time, depending who you ask). So everyone wants to be buried near the spot where they will all be brought back to life. Jesus walked over this hill and through that important gate every day to preach inside the city during the last week of his life, which is one of the reasons for the whole son-of-God thing.

Omri took us up to the Mount of Olives to start the day for a reason: he wanted to give us the history of the city, and that history was totally tied to the geography that we could see from the top of this important hill.

"Do you see that low point, down there, with the trees?" Omri said, pointing.

We did.

"That's a natural spring. That's why the first people settled here, for the water. Next, they built their temple. In Roman times, they built temples on the highest place above the water source."

We could see that the Temple Mount is indeed the highest place above the water source.

"So, it was the most important place in town. So then Abraham went there to almost slay his son. So then Mohammed flew there overnight from Mecca on his way up to heaven. So now the Jewish temple must be built there or else no Messiah and so on and so on," Omri finished up.

All that fighting, all because of geography.

The city of Jerusalem has a law that all buildings must be made of the creamy, gorgeous Jerusalem stones that were used to build the ancient city, so the entire city is white and turns colors with the sunrise and sunset. The one building that is not white is in the middle of it all— the blue and gold mosque on the Temple Mount. Despite this being the most contentious building in the world, it looks fantastic surrounded by all of that Israeli stone. It's my opinion that if the two sides could just focus on the pleasing aesthetic their two cultures have produced in this city, as well as their mutual love of hummus, we could solve this thing.

We continued into the city, making way for pilgrims walking the stations of the cross with an actual cross on their backs, posing for pictures in front of Arab shops under the weight of their crucifixes. We got Omri's viewpoint of the events of the city. He told us amazing stories, like one about a ladder that was left on the roof of the Church of the Holy Sepulchre, which stands on the spot where Jesus was crucified. Every sect of Christians shares ownership of this church, and they fight amongst each other over who gets to sweep which step as viciously as the Jews fight the Muslims. A Muslim family down the road is the keeper of the keys to the front door of the holiest church in Christendom, because none of the Christians can stomach any of the *other* Christians having it. The story goes that a ladder was once left on top of the church, and no sect would take responsibility for leaving it there. And so the ladder stayed on top of the church for *sixty years.*

Jerusalem did not discourage my belief that religion makes people crazy.

I loved that day. I always say that I need to travel to keep from dying of boredom from my own internal monologue. I think that, generally, most of us have a total of about twenty thoughts. And we just scroll through those thoughts, over and over again, in varying order, all day every day. Maybe your twenty are much more interesting than this, but mine include: "I should call my mom." "Am I any good at my job?" "Why do I still get neck acne?" "Why don't I either call my mom or not call my mom but stop wasting energy on feeling guilty if I don't call her?" Et cetera.

Now, if I don't leave town, *that's it*. Those are my thoughts. That's what I've got to keep me warm at night. And good Yahweh does that get boring.

When you travel you're forced to have new thoughts. "Is this alley safe?" "Is this the right bus?" "Was this meat ever a house pet?" It doesn't even matter what the new thoughts are, it feels so good to just have some variety. And it's a reboot for your brain. I can feel the neurons making new connections again with new problems to solve, clawing their way back to their nimbler, younger days. Even the process of learning about Israel, let alone my day in Jerusalem, woke up my thought patterns again better than anywhere I've ever been. I love that place for that.

After our day with Omri, we went home and covered up for our Orthodox Shabbat dinner with my friend's family. Donning tights, long skirts, and newly purchased long-sleeved black tops, we put our lust-provoking hair in a bun, and tried to turn ourselves into visions of modesty.

We stopped by the Western Wall on our way to dinner, which we were told began at 6:52 (sunset). The Western Wall just before sunset on a Friday is a magnificent scene to behold. Women praying on one side, men praying on the other, mothers reaching over the wall to hand things to their sons. The sound of it all is incredible, too. So many people's voices raised in prayer and song, and, drifting over it all, music from another Friday-night event in Jerusalem's Old City: Arab weddings.

Astrid and I stuck some wishes in the wall, and then joined the masses on their sunset parade up the hundreds of ancient stone steps from the Western Wall to the Jewish Quarter. Now, let's remember we were in the most deeply conservative Jewish neighborhood in the world. In their holiest spot. On the holiest night of the week. It's all wigs and black suits and furry hats. But about halfway up the staircase, a woman in a wig tapped on Astrid's shoulder and pointed down at my friend's rear. And that's when we realized that, with each step, Astrid had been stepping on the hem of her floor-length, sadly elastic-waisted skirt such that it had been yanked all the way down to her upper thighs. So thousands of Orthodox Jews who are not allowed to shake women's hands got a view of my blond *shiksa* friend's thong-clad booty. She mooned the Western Wall on Shabbat.

We tried.

After Astrid turned the other butt cheek, we made our way through the stone alleyways to the home of my Californian friend's cousin Rachel. We walked into Rachel's home, and forgetting, I held out my hand to shake hands with her husband . . . who of course can't touch women. He grinned, and said in his thick Russian accent, "I can't shake your hand, but you're very welcome here," and I put my hand down, apologizing.

Rachel had grown up as a secular Jew in Indiana, but

had become very religious in her twenties. While at yeshiva (religious school) in New York, she got set up with a Russian man who was living in Canada, and who had also only become Orthodox as an adult. They met a few times, decided to marry, and moved to Jerusalem, where they had "only" five children. Astrid and I obviously thought the whole thing was insane . . . except they seemed *really* happy and peaceful with each other, laughing a lot and finishing each other's sentences affectionately.

"*He* wasn't afraid to make a promise to a woman," Astrid pointed out.

"They jumped in so fast there wasn't any time to make pro/con lists," I said. "Not the worst thing in the world."

More fascinating, though, was that Rachel was a former journalist who wrote a book about the Jewish laws governing the woman's domain of home, sex, and marriage, and so often found herself counseling women on sexual issues. Rachel's husband had trained her in some therapeutic techniques for this purpose, since he was a therapist who developed a Torah-based brand of therapy, which also included modern psychotherapeutic techniques, hypnotherapy, and past-life regression. There were several paintings around their small apartment of rainbow-hued swirls that he said were painted by *different* patients to describe what the past-life regression process looks like. They all looked almost identical.

He does this therapy for people all over the world, sometimes via Skype, in his black top hat and long beard from his little stone pad in Jerusalem. I asked him if he thought he could do the past-life regressing to me.

"Oh, yes, it is much easier to do to non-Jews," he said.

"Why is that?"

"Because you don't have as many hang-ups. Jews come out of the regression therapy wanting to change, but there's still these hundreds of rules we all have to follow every day. It makes real growth and change difficult. It's easier for the nonreligious," he said.

Now, I have a wing of Republican born-again Christians in my family. They are lovely people, but we are not cut from the same cloth sociopolitically. I've always said I'd be happy to be married by a rabbi if I married a Jew, but that I could never under any circumstances get married in a church. It just represents too much of a belief system I've rejected. Plus, Jews don't try to recruit you—you're either one or you're not, which I appreciate.

But I gotta say, I got a new perspective on that Jesus guy during my day walking in his footsteps through the Hasidic neighborhoods of Jerusalem. Even as a nonbeliever, it was suddenly really easy to imagine what it must have felt like to be a Jew at the start of the first millennium, subjected to several hundred laws and restrictions that, if broken, could lead to, say, a stoning or, at the very least, a stern shunning. And then here comes this great-looking hippie rabbi in sandals saying, "Just love your neighbor, forgive and forget, and you're good." No wonder the message was so powerful. Like the Hasidic hypnotist-therapist said, it's *hard* to be an Orthodox Jew.

There were many people visiting Rachel's family for the Shabbat dinner, which I thought would be staid and serious, what with all the praying and holiness and all. But it was actually very warm and raucous. While the therapist prayed, food was passed and stories were told and Arabic music from the wedding down the lane floated in the windows that offered a view of the Temple Mount. Rachel's thirteen-year-old son cheerfully explained the reasons for all of the rituals:

"Listen, we wash our hands three times because the people who only washed their hands one time all died of the plague. And guess what—we're still here."

The women sat on one end of the table, and the men on the other, and there were several other foreigners visiting for dinner who were strangers to the family. Teaching outsiders about Shabbat dinner is something this family apparently does often, and they were funny and friendly with all of us. There were three twenty-year-old girls who had grown up in nonreligious American households, but had each become Orthodox, brought themselves alone to Israel, and, in some cases, had lost their families over it. This family was taking them all in.

Rachel showed me her book about the family purity guidelines for Orthodox women, and told me that because of it so many women sit at her side of the Shabbat table and lean in close to ask her questions that are always about one subject: sex. *Do the thing you're supposed to do in the place you're supposed to do it.* So I leaned in close, and while her husband thumbed through his Torah on the male side of the table, I asked her about love and sex. I told her about my life, and the obsessive and extensive pro/con lists I'd mentally kept (and sometimes physically transcribed) on everyone I've ever dated, and then asked her about how the Orthodox community goes about this whole song and dance.

She told me that since they date exclusively with the intent to marry, the conversation is very direct right from the start. You're not sitting quietly next to each other at a movie wondering if you can get over his awful shirt. You're interviewing. And from your first date, you're focusing, apparently, on only three questions:

Do we want the same things out of life?

Do we bring out the best in each other?

Do we find each other attractive?

That's it. *In that order.* You're not allowed to marry someone you don't find attractive, *by religious decree,* but it's *third* on the list. And Rachel said that because you aren't getting physical with each other, which "muddles you up emotionally so you don't know which way is up or down," it's all very cut-and-dried, and so the process can happen very quickly. You also usually meet someone through a friend or a professional matchmaker, so you do extensive research about a possible mate before even meeting him, asking his rabbi and his neighbors, his teachers and his friends, all about him. Then, if you find him attractive, and some sparks fly, it's safe—you already know he's a good, solid person.

"That way you don't end up in bed with some handsome guy you meet at a party, and then discover the next day that he's all about money and you're all about saving the world, but because you're all jumbled up about his looks and the sex, you keep dating him anyway for a year or two before you break up with him because he's all about money," Rachel clarified.

Astrid and I looked at each other, nodding.

I asked her about the love question—if you get married a few dates into meeting someone, you clearly can't love them yet. You're just betting that you someday will. I told her about how I had spent my adult life saying the same thing: *I'm not looking for a particular person, I'm looking for a particular feeling.* I wanted to *feel* over-the-moon in love with someone. I thought that was how I would know he was The One. So I found it amazing that couples were committing their *lives* to each other before they knew each other well enough to know if they could love each other.

"In Judaism, the way you learn to love someone is by giving to them," she said. "The more you give to a person, the more you end up loving them. If love is just a feeling, and that feeling changes, then what? Love has to be something you choose to build."

She also talked about why she thinks that a higher percentage of religious marriages are happy than nonreligious: they have all of these rules to follow that basically lead to them working really, really hard on their marriages. Start with the fact that all Jews are supposed to be spending their lives bettering themselves, becoming as Godly as humanly possible. And then on top of that, men *have* to please their wives sexually. It's an order from the greatest sages. It's also best, mitzvah-wise, if they please their wives *before* they are pleased themselves. You also *can't* speak evil about your mate. You *have* to treat each other with kindness, and you *must* get down there and float your lady's boat, and you *can't* bad-mouth each other, even to your friends over a nice glass of pinot. *God forbids it.*

"Plus, men can't touch us for two weeks out of the month, so when you have those two weeks together in one bed, it's always really exciting," she added. "And for those other two weeks, you have to find ways to connect that aren't sexual, which is so important, too."

It was all pretty interesting. And then, after I talked about my deep ambivalence about marriage, mostly because I feared giving up my freedom, she said something that really stuck:

"The deep feeling of oneness you have with someone when you've done all of the work on yourself you have to do to make a marriage work doesn't take away your independence. It frees you to be the person you actually are. It wipes away all that nasty ego stuff, and lets your soul shine through."

As much as I adored this woman, my favorite person at the table was her fifteen-year-old daughter. She was a volunteer first-response medic, important in a city of narrow walking streets where ambulances can't drive, and she planned on becoming a nurse one day. (The religious women usually work, because many of the Orthodox men spend much of their lives in religious study.) But she had another hobby that really made her light up: boxing. This was a real surprise.

"Do you box with girls? Boys aren't allowed to touch you, right?" I asked.

"I box with nonreligious boys. I got permission from

the rabbi because it's therapeutic," she explained lightly. I didn't probe.

It turned out that she boxed with boys in her long skirt five days a week, four hours a day, with a male sixty-year-old coach she loved like a father. I dug this girl—she was spunky and smart and tough.

"You're *Million Shekel Baby*," I told her, which of course she didn't get.

She got married two years later, at seventeen, just like she'd always planned. She married a boy who was eight years her senior, who had kind of adopted her family as his own because he was an only child from a nonreligious family. He was a regular at their Shabbat dinner for more than a year before starting to date their daughter. He thought she was older than she was, she thought he was younger, but the family loved him, and I hear they are very happy. They had their first daughter almost immediately. *Million Shekel Baby* doesn't box anymore.

Now, do I wish I got married at seventeen? Do I hope my daughter gets married at seventeen? Of course not. But these women were certainly doing a lot less internal wrestling than Astrid and I were. And seeing how happy they were in marriages that in no way started with that "feeling," but, somehow, over the years, grew into plenty of feelings that sounded deep and rich and happy . . . that stuck with me.

I could write about Israel forever. I even ended up going back just three weeks later, on a free trip I amazingly got offered during my first visit. In exchange for the trip, I spoke at a film festival, and taught some Israeli film students about sitcom writing, helping them write jokes in a second language. It was during the Turkish flotilla crisis, and so partway through my trip they moved me to a kibbutz that was out of missile range of Gaza, and when I was introduced at the festival, they also informed the audience of the location of the closest bomb shelter. The Israeli comedy writers drove an hour to hear me speak, shrugging off the crisis. Israelis are some of the best in the world at living in the moment, and shrugging off possible disaster. Statistically they are also some of the happiest, which I believe is directly connected.

I had to leave a week earlier than I planned from my second trip to Israel because I got a job—on *Chuck*, my first nonsitcom, a totally new kind of show for me. At the interview, I gushed about Israel, about the Mossad (*Chuck* was an international spy show), and about all of the things I had learned from all of the people I'd met. I got the job, and it opened up a new avenue for work that is still reaping rewards, and it happened partially because of the stories I came home with from Israel.

Argentina was the first place that reenergized my life. It would always be my special place because it had been the first, but Israel reminded me that there were thousands of places out there still. And discovering them would always be my way out of the blues. While slow careerwise, the previous year and a half was the best travel period of my life: six weeks in New Zealand, three in Australia, one in Iceland, one in Chamonix, three in Israel. Comedy was dead, but my travel schedule was hopping. Israel rebooted my brain, and made me interested in my life again.

Now, on that first Israeli trip, did I change my flight, like always, and stay an extra week after Astrid left? I did. And was it less than twenty-four hours after her plane lifted off the tarmac before I was sleeping with a Yemeni-Israeli soldier/bartender named Inon? Yes. Did he introduce himself over his kosher bar with raised eyebrows and a pointed, *"My name is IN. ON."*? Yes again. Did he ultimately end up, in fact, *in* me while I was *on* his kitchen counter? Also yes. Listen, if I haven't made it clear by now, you meet people quickly when you're alone. But, on this trip, the boys were just an endnote.

12

······························

"Juan More Time, with Feeling" (Argentina, Part 3)

Los Angeles International → Cartagena Rafael Nuñez
International → Buenos Aires Ezeiza
Departing: April 2, 2011

There is an actual medical condition called Jerusalem Syndrome. Each year, it afflicts hundreds of people when they go to Israel and are so religiously moved that they become convinced God is speaking to them, and that they are the Messiah. There is a dedicated wing in the psychiatric ward at a hospital in Jerusalem that deals with these people. I met a psychiatrist who works there, and asked her what the treatment is.

"It is easiest if there is more than one patient in the

clinic at a time," she told me. "The best way to snap them out of it is usually to introduce them to each other."

I love that image—the guy who is sure he's the Messiah meeting *another* guy who is sure *he's* the Messiah, and immediately going, "Oh. Well, that guy sounds crazy. Never mind."

I experienced that at an apartment party one night in Los Angeles. Hope and I were holding red plastic cups filled with keg beer, and getting the dancing started while scanning the living room for cute boys. I looked over at my thirty-*cough*-year-old dancing friend whom I had watched doing this precise set of activities for so many decades, and was hit by a not-particularly-insightful insight.

"We have been doing this for a *really* long time."

That set us off on a fit of hysterical laughter, but it was not exclusively funny. My friends and I were getting old for all of this.

I was also starting to notice that, just like Astrid, a lot of my beautiful, smart, well-traveled girlfriends, who claimed that they ultimately wanted to get married and have kids, were still exclusively picking very handsome younger men who told them at the outset of their relationships that they were not interested in a commitment. My friends would ignore these facts, and their relationships would eventually implode. They also turned down dates with reasonable, not-quite-so-adorable available men.

Being face-to-face with the mirror that all of this added up to kind of snapped me out of it. *Oh, well, that sounds crazy. Never mind.*

I also spent New Year's 2011 in Chamonix, in a

gorgeous chalet filled with comedians. It was a lovely, enchanted, European white wonderland, and they were *loud*. So loud. You can't imagine how badly they all needed to tell *so* many jokes *so* many hours per day. It was the dick-joke Olympics. While the sheer amount of laughter was a delight, there was a tonnage issue, and I finally decided that *funny* was not only no longer a priority for me in the Potential Guy Department, it was maybe something to be avoided. *Interesting* and *witty* and, mostly, *calm* were now at the top of the have-to-have list.

I was also not ready to follow the advice of a book Sasha was currently recommending to me, *Marry Him: The Case for Settling for Mr. Good Enough*. That, I hope we can all agree, is the most depressing advice any woman has ever uttered. I once heard the author of this book speak, and this was her story: she had been an attractive woman who had tons of choices in men. No one was "good enough." She turned forty, and her choices were gone, and she made a sperm-bank baby. She wished she had settled earlier, since she felt her age meant she wasn't even marketable enough to settle for anything reasonable anymore. She claims women who are thirty and say they aren't worried about getting married are lying. Her main message: *Settle while you're young enough to settle for pretty good.*

Kill me. And, please, someone help this woman have some fun.

So I was looking for a third option.

That third option was taking a while to find, so I decided to freeze my eggs. A little on that decision: It had occurred to me many years earlier that I grab, smooch, and adore every small child that comes within a ten-foot radius of me. (Aside from the shitty ones.) I had been in the delivery room for the birth of Sasha's daughter that year, and had spent the following week wandering around in a daze, daydreaming about that little girl like I would daydream about a new boyfriend. The intense infatuation I had with that baby taught me that I did not have to be genetically connected to a tiny person to be madly in love with it. I needed to bond and shape more than I needed to grow and push. So I relaxed about the biology thing, happy to adopt if I didn't end up settling down until after my ovaries had decided to retire to Florida. (I just had an image of my retired ovaries, driving around Boca in a huge eighties Cadillac, shaking their little ovarian fists at crazy young motorcyclists. And . . . scene.)

Anyway, I then remembered that not all men might be as happy to adopt. And that putting some future babies in the fridge might not only be a way around a possible deal breaker, but it could be something great to do for the man with whom I someday settled down. I certainly was not going to wait this long to find the perfect person and then rush into making a baby just because of biology. I had watched many formerly picky and thoughtful friends lose their minds and do exactly this as they hit their late thirties, rushing into the creation of a new, possibly relationship-ruining life. So, feeling exactly like when I set up my first 401(k), I set up my egg-freezing, a lady in the new millennium taking care of herself.

My mother was *delighted*. She wept and laughed and clapped her hands like I'd told her I was pregnant. It was just such a relief to her that I at least was *planning* on the baby thing, finally, like a regular person. (My stepfather, a doctor, had often received calls from me over the years requesting that he phone in a renewal of my birth-control prescription. Often I would hear my mother shout, "Don't give them to her!" sassily in the background. The woman wanted me knocked up, bad.) So, she cheered me on as I started my little science experiment on myself, injecting things into my body, growing breasts that looked like they could feed the metropolitan area. My mom dropped me off after egg-retrieval day with a list of fifteen baby names, one for every egg I retrieved. (Jazzy Newman was one option, short for Jasmine. So, a stripper.)

Of course, just like in a J-Lo movie, as soon as I started the fertility injections, I met a guy. He was a moody, sensitive TV editor with great eyelashes who kept me on my toes rationalizing several pieces of information, dispensed over a few months:

1. He had made a documentary about a sex commune in San Francisco, as part of his "exploration of whether or not monogamy makes sense."
2. He had cheated on his ex-wife, who, it turned out, I had met before.
3. He announced he was ready to stop seeing other people months after I assumed we had both stopped seeing other people.

But I pushed past all of these data points, and kept going, my head down. I was the Little Engine Who Could Ignore Massive Red Flags.

And I quietly went forward with freezing my eggs. Which led to mystifying days where I injected fertility drugs into my stomach in the morning, and then had sex with my boyfriend with a condom later that night. *Might there be an easier way?* a modern girl might ask herself. Eventually, when I had to call off sexy time for a couple of weeks because of the procedure, I told him what I was doing. He reacted calmly.

"That's cool. It's like the opposite of the talk I usually get from women your age. It means you *aren't* in a hurry."

The news also, mysteriously, made this guy who was absolutely not in a hurry suddenly *really* anxious to stick things in me without a condom, even though that could have turned into dozen-tuplets. I think my fertility phere-mones were intoxicating.

I ended up with a couple of handfuls of little potential babies in the freezer. (The doctor said I had "gorgeous lin-ing" and that *if I were younger* I would have "donor ova-ries." The doctor's voice had a very smooth-jazz kind of purr to it, so this sounded sexier when he said it.) Anyway, I thought my life was going just great, until one night a couple of months later, when the editor and I were taking a bath.

We sat in the two-person tub I had purchased in an optimistic "if you build it they will come" sort of mood. I had then sat in it alone for a year, until my bath-loving boyfriend came along. On the bathing night in question, there were bubbles and candles and rose petals and wine. (On a Wednesday! Sometimes I'm awesome.) We climbed in, and chatted about our day, and I rubbed his feet, and then he told me he had been obsessively listening to a song that made him think about me. *Awwwwww*, I said, super naked. But he continued.

The song was called "The Curse." *Awwwwww?* It was about a zombie who comes to life when he falls in love with a beautiful girl. For a while they walk the earth together, alive and in love, but eventually it becomes clear that his liveliness has only occurred as a result of his zombie nature—he went ahead and sucked out the beautiful girl's life force. So she starts to wither and gray and ultimately must go to bed a shell of her former self. He then leaves her and dates other live women.

So I stood up and climbed out of the tub, more naked than I've ever been, picked the rose petals off my bubbly body, and we broke up. In the morning, I woke up with that *"Shit, I'm single again"* feeling, walked into the bathroom, and found a tub with dead rose petals stuck to the bottom of it. They reminded me of confetti and cigarette-filled cups on the floor after the party is all over.

And so I e-mailed Father Juan.

Juan and I had stayed in touch after his visit the previous year. He had even invited me to come skiing in Patagonia with his family (*!!!!*) a couple of months before the bathtub breakup, but I had a life-force-sucking boyfriend, and a job. I had been *really* grateful that I had the job, which kept me from looking too closely at what my answer to Juan would have been if it was just the moody nonmonogamous bather standing in between me and a trip to Juan's beautiful family's beautiful ski cabin in freaking Patagonia.

Anyway, after the breakup, there were a few more months filled with e-mail flirting with Juan, and writing a show about a nerdy spy with a supercomputer in his brain, and my annual-yet-now-age-inappropriate Christmas road trip in the backseat of my mommy's husband's car with my pillow and blankie. And then, after all of that, because I really, really deserved it, the mother lode was delivered unto me:

RE: COLOMBIA????

Hola, Pulpa!!!!! I go alone for three week trip to Colombia in Avril for to take pictures.........maybe you can come???????? Will be days to know us better...
　　Beso muy grande,
　　Dulce de leche!!!!!

It can be argued that *Romancing the Stone* messed me up pretty good. Sexy Michael Douglas, with that hat, and that smile, chopping off Kathleen Turner's high heels, fighting off jungle guerillas, wrestling crocodiles, and then dancing her around a courtyard in white linen before showing up on her doorstep in a boat and sailing her off through the streets of New York happily ever after? That's intoxicating stuff . . . and nonexistent.

But that is exactly what I expected out of my Colombian adventure with Father Juan.

I stopped eating. I lasered/waxed/dermabrased everything. I dragged the *Chuck* writing staff to the gym at Warner Bros. every day at lunch. I listened to Spanish lessons in the car. I bought a lot of white linen, and turquoise jewelry that I hoped would "pop" on the golden skin I got for forty-five dollars in Beverly Hills. I dyed my eyelashes for model-like emergences from the ocean. I procured sexy jammies that lifted my girls up a little higher than they were naturally perching these days. No Colombian guerilla has ever brought out bigger guns. Or higher ones.

Because I was not merely meeting Juan in Colombia. He also invited me to come back with him to Argentina, where I would be staying in his apartment for three more weeks. We were going to go to his friend's wedding, and to Argentine wine country in Mendoza, and to his family's Arabian-horse ranch out in the pampas for *Semana Santa* (Easter Week). I was not going to be in Buenos Aires in an apartment checking my phone to see if Juan had called. I was going to be moving in.

Now, I was 87 percent sure that this was just going to be another great vacation with a great guy. But . . . *six years*. We had been finding each other for *six years*. Sure, I was a godless TV writer and he was an almost-priest who lived a continent away. Absolutely, my friends and family were looking at me skeptically and asking questions like, "Are you sure you want to do this?" But that made the fact that we kept coming back to each other after all these years even *more* amazing, right? And there was something different in his voice and his eyes now when we Skyped. He was starting to wonder if this was something, too.

"*Ah, que linda sos,*" he would coo over the computer. *How pretty you are.*

"Will be days to know us better . . ."

Because of work I could only meet him for the final week of his three weeks in Colombia. I left the earliest minute I could. My last day at *Chuck* was spent in the Hollywood Hills, under the Hollywood sign, filming a scene from an episode I wrote that was meant to take place in a mining town deep in the mountains of—you guessed it— Colombia. That's how you write off a trip, ladies and gentlemen! So on the day I left to meet Father Juan, I woke up at dawn to get my hair blown out, then spent the day on my set shooting a fake Colombia that hundreds of people built because I told them to, then left at midnight to go meet my Argentine lover in the real Colombia, groomed to within an inch of my life. It was the most glamorous I've ever been.

On the plane, I sat between two solo travelers in their midtwenties. She was on her way to her friend's wedding in Cartagena, he was on his way to have his first solo backpacking adventure. We all ordered drinks, and then they chatted over me as I tried to breathe and control my fantasies of living happily-ever-after with Juan on the pampas. By the end of the flight they had exchanged numbers, and were going to share a cab into town. I felt like the postgrads at the end of *St. Elmo's Fire*, when they see the college kids in their bar and decide to go home early and meet up for brunch instead.

"We are beginning our descent into Cartagena . . ."

I checked my lip gloss while my internal monologue picked up speed:

What if I split my time between Los Angeles and Buenos Aires, and Juan and I get married and have babies and we all become fluent in Spanish? That wouldn't be the boring, scary version of settling down that gives me panic attacks. That would be an amazing, fantastic Diane Lane movie. "Hey, did you hear about Kristin Newman? She married some hot Argentine priest, and they had three gorgeous babies who speak like ten languages, and she sells a movie a year and lives on a campo in Argentina! She totally did it!"

My seat partners were peeking at each other over me, exchanging flirty little smiles.

"Welcome to Colombia . . ."

Juan was waiting for me at the airport. His big white smile was framed by a few days of scruff and a backpacker's tan that shone beautifully in the oppressive humidity.

"Pulpa," he said as he pulled me into his chest.

Four weeks later, I found myself hugging Juan in an airport once again.

"Pulpa," he said, in a totally different tone of voice.

"I'll always be grateful we did this," I said, crying onto his neck.

"I will remember you forever," Juan promised. "You'll come visit me with your family someday," he whispered into my ear.

Tears streaming down my face, I walked away from the

exquisite Father Juan for the last time, and got on the first of my two seven-hour plane rides home to my cat.

Now, I know that was abrupt, finding out how it was all going to turn out before hearing the whole story. But the thing about this last trip with the man who was my most important vacation romance was that *I* found out how it was all going to turn out before hearing the whole story, too. I knew that I was not going to be living happily-ever-after on the pampas after only a couple of days in Colombia.

On our first day in Cartagena, Juan and I were giddy, holding hands and giggling with wonder that we had made this all happen. We strolled through the steamy cobbled streets, he continued to glimmer beautifully, and I continued to turn into a splotchy red tomato in a white dress. The northern Europeans just do not handle heat as attractively as the tanner varietals.

We had gone to our hotel room first, and the air-conditioning inside felt remarkable, but the big bed really filled that little room, and we were not quite ready for its implications. Our hotel was also called Casa de la Fey—House of Faith—and there were Catholic icons decorating the place that made us both want to explore outside a bit first.

We caught up on our year apart, and had mojitos and ceviche, and took pictures in front of the dozens of gorgeous old painted doors and flower-strewn balconies of Cartagena. We ran into the girl from the plane, who giggled when she saw Juan, and told me that she had a date to see our third seatmate later that night. The sun set, and we went to a bar set up outside on top of the old fortress walls, and kissed above the pink and orange Caribbean in the warm, salty wind. It was good. The magic was still there.

We went back to our room to change for dinner, and he pulled out a crisp white linen shirt that he had been keeping clean for our first night in Colombia. He was doing his part for my *Romancing the Stone* fantasy. He also surprised me by pulling out a T-shirt he had brought especially for me. It was the shirt he was wearing the first night we met six years earlier, at that party outside Buenos Aires. I remembered it because of pictures, but I couldn't believe that he did. For the first time ever, I felt like that night meant as much to him as it had to me.

And, finally, relaxed and a drink in, we fell into bed and made love before dinner. And it was . . .

. . . not spectacular. And if you think you heard a little drumroll in your head between those sets of ellipses, imagine the epic drum solo I had been hearing for the previous year and a half. The sex wasn't bad, it was just all a little awkward. Not like the year before in Los Angeles. The kisses were missing something, and I started to have a little *uh-oh* feeling. But I told myself it was so loaded, this first sex after a year, after so many flights, with so many expectations. Expectations were always my undoing. So we took a shower (a spectacular thing to do with Father Juan) and went out for dinner in a cobbled square very much like where Michael Douglas danced with Kathleen Turner.

A couple more days of sexy travel greatness ensued, and then we took off for Parque Tayrona, a national park made up of pristine, desolate jungles and beaches on the Caribbean. On the way we stopped at Volcan Totumo, a bizarre mud volcano that you immerse yourself in. It looks like a hundred-foot-high termite hill, and sits on the banks of a river in the middle of nowhere. A staircase has been built up the side of it, and at the top you find a caldera of perfectly smooth, warm, gooey mud. It's very viscous, so you float easily in any position, like you're perching in pudding. Also floating with you are Colombian men who give you massages as you hover in the goo together.

Juan and I painted each other's bodies and faces with mud, and then got massaged, and then walked down to the banks of the river, where women stripped off our swimsuits and scrubbed us clean like we were little babies. After they got the mud out of our hidden spots, they toweled us off while their children played nearby. It was the most unusual spa experience I've ever had, and cost two dollars. It would be hard to decide which I enjoyed more: getting my thighs rubbed in warm mud, or painting Juan. My version of Sophie's choice.

At Parque Tayrona, we stayed in a small collection of gorgeous little cabanas in the national park, where alligators lounged on the beach and fully weaponized *policía* checked your papers. It was spectacular, our little place, and the vision of Juan stretched out on the white beach lounge hanging from two palm trees is a sight I will never forget. He carved "PULPA" into a walking stick for me. We spent the days walking down so many beaches that we'd run out of daylight before we got home, and I'd end up rock-climbing at night in the Colombian jungle in a bikini, using my iPhone flashlight app for light as I scrambled away from the breaking waves. But it was while on those beautiful beaches that I knew for sure that this was, indeed, just another vacation romance.

We ran out of things to talk about. While hunting for topics, religion obviously came up, and his time at the seminary, and so we got into that in a real way for the first time. I found it fascinating to hear about the life of a seminarian, and enjoyed being educated on the lives of the saints, but I was also honest about what I believed was historic fact and what I considered to be myth. I told him about how I longed to be a believer, because believers seemed so much calmer than I had ever been about anything, but I just hadn't seen the evidence that could convince me. Juan wasn't pushy about his beliefs, but I could tell he saw my lack of faith as a little sad. He asked if I ever wanted to get baptized "just in case." I asked if he thought Jesus would have been anything more than a world-changing ethicist if he had lived during the era of Internet fact-checking or flash photography.

But the *aha-ohno* moment for me really came when we were strolling down the empty beach, and Juan, in slooooow sentences, told me the story of the two sets of footsteps in the sand that turned into one when Jesus was carrying the first dude during his times of trouble. You know the one—from the Hallmark Special Moments posters. I nodded as he told the tale, and pretended I had never heard it before, or made fun of it before, and knew this beautiful man was not mine.

I would find out that I wasn't his, either. I spin too fast, he moves too slow, I like to tease and joke and criticize and judge, he has an internal light radiating out of him for all of God's creatures. My Internet password is my cat's name, his is his favorite saint's.

But we didn't talk about any of that on the Colombian beach. Have I mentioned how important it is to me to have a great vacation? And you saw just earlier in this chapter with the bather how adept I can be at putting my head down and ignoring unpleasant facts. So I just felt a brief moment of loss as I listened to the footsteps story, and then I got down to the business of doing what I had spent my adult life mastering—enjoying a relationship that I knew was going to last only as long as my vacation. My internal pep talk sounded about like this:

You are in a beautiful place with a beautiful guy. You have a month to go. You like each other. Amazing experiences are going to happen, here and in Argentina. Be grateful and enjoy him. Have fun.

And you know what? I did.

It was while on the plane from Colombia to Argentina, while Juan and I snuggled on each other's shoulders, that I came as close as I dared to discussing the reality of what was going on between us.

"I know I'm staying with you a really long time," I said. "If it's too much, or you need space, I can spend some of the time with other friends, so just tell me."

"Okay," he said simply. Not *No way.* Not *Of course not.*

It's hard to describe what it felt like to see Juan's apartment for the first time. It grounded this sort of mythical person for me. It made him real. *He lives in an apartment.*

This is where he brushes his teeth. This is what kind of couch he likes. This is where he's been all this time.

The minute we walked in, he felt different. A little chillier, a little less relaxed. His vacation was over. We were no longer in the bubble of *pretend* and *away*. He told me the stories behind his family photos, and we went out to get pizza at the neighborhood joint, but he seemed distracted, and farther away.

The next day, we went to his friend's wedding. I met the people he'd known since childhood, who all adored him, and were fantastic-looking and friendly and completely fascinated by the news that Juan had had an American girl in his life for six years. We danced at the reception, and spent the weekend at one of his family's weekend country houses, where I lay by the pool and Juan trimmed the pomegranate trees and cousins stopped by, and it was all so great that my certainty that he and I were a nonstarter faded a bit. We had such a good time together. It felt so good to be with these people. Everyone was *so good-looking.* Oh, and did I mention that the name of Juan's family's weekend-home community was *"NEWMAN"*? We spent the weekend in NEWMAN, Argentina. So, the country club was called Club NEWMAN. The kids all went to a school called NEWMAN. The horse stables were called NEWMAN. Juan and I strolled down to a rugby match one day and all of the gorgeous Argentine rugby players were wearing jerseys with NEWMAN across their backs. *This place literally had my name all over it.* MOO-COW!!! MOO-COW!!!

When we went back to Buenos Aires, we threw dinner

parties in his apartment, and made breakfast together, and I taught him how to cook a few of my specialties that I hadn't found the time to cook in the States in about ten years. We pretended we were a happy little couple.

But . . . it sure was quiet over breakfast. And did I mention that I was initiating sex 100 percent of the time? Oh, and then there was the time that we ran into a priest friend of his, and then, an hour later, the priest called to ask Juan if he would like to be set up on a date with the priest's sister.

"I told him no," Juan said, blushing as he hung up the phone and I cooked. "I've seen his sister."

"I'm living with a man who priests hope will date their sisters," I e-mailed my mom. I didn't even discuss the other element—the priest had met me, and hadn't for even a moment thought Juan and I were together. And Juan hadn't turned the setup down because of anything having to do with me, either.

I also met Juan's mother and grandmother, gracious, lovely women who lived together with their maid in a beautiful apartment down the street from Juan. And then, a few days into my time in Argentina, Juan's grandmother was hospitalized. It looked bad, like she wouldn't make it, and so family started to fly in from all over the world to say good-bye.

Now . . . how does one handle a dying grandmother when one is trying to be in a short-term vacationship that one's partner may or may not want to be in? Did Juan want me to disappear? Or hold his hand at the bedside vigil?

"Cook," my mother commanded over e-mail. "Cook

for everyone. Bring it to the hospital. That's what Latin women expect."

I asked Juan if he wanted me to leave, or stay, or help, or cook. He didn't really give me any feedback, as usual. "Do what you like," was about all I ever got.

So I cooked. I dropped by with food. I met lots of relatives, from all over the world, who looked very interested in the fact that Juan had an American girl by his side at his grandmother's deathbed. And then I cleared out, meeting up with my other friends in the city, taking tango classes, giving Juan space in case I wasn't welcome. It was awkward.

Juan's grandmother eventually recovered, and lived for almost another year, it turned out. She was a very gentle, smiley woman, who gave great hugs, and had cool cheeks that smelled like lavender, and held my hand when we chatted. I'm glad I brought food to her hospital room.

At the end of my month in South America, the first of my two seven-hour flights home to Los Angeles got me to Panama, where I made a beeline for a bookstore. The AV system had been broken on the first flight, and I had finished reading my only book, and was terrified of another seven-hour flight without distraction. Panicking when I couldn't find an English-language book in the entire airport, I headed for the ticket counter, where I confirmed that there were indeed movies on the next flight to Los Angeles.

"I really, really need them," I said to the flight attendant.

"Okay," she said. "Next?"

I was sick to my stomach. I was no longer the girl with an Argentine lover. Now I was just alone, and thirty-seven, and going home to get back on Match.com. It was only in that moment that I realized what a life raft Juan had been for me all of those years alone on my couch, even when we weren't in contact. He was out there. He made me different. He was a possibility, a *maybe, just maybe*. And that was now over.

I bought a calling card, found a phone, and then, heart racing, I reached out across the continents and spilled my story to the girl who could always make me feel better.

"I really need you," I said to Hope.

"Tell me," she said, like always.

Hope had spent a couple of years in South America in high school and college, and loved it long before I did, so she knew exactly what I was describing as I told her about my month in Argentina with Juan's friends and family. The delicious feeling of being *part of it*, of really living a normal life in a totally exotic place.

Juan's family had a campo, or a ranch, about five hours outside Buenos Aires. It had been in the family for generations, and his aunt and uncle raised soybeans and Arabian horses there. His uncle, a doctor in Buenos Aires, raced the horses on eight-hour endurance races even in his seventies, and riders from all over the world would come to his campo to buy his horses.

Juan had described this place to me many times over

the years, in ways that made me ache for my fantasy bicontinental life:

RE: ¡Feliz Año Nuevo!

My new year was spent on the campo with many childrens and horses, as it should be......If you come to Argentina we must make a visit to here!!!!!!

My last week in Argentina, Juan took me out to the campo for *Semana Santa*. We drove out with his welcoming, interesting aunt and uncle, and his cousin's twelve-year-old daughter. She was chatty and adorable, and we traded Spanish and English lessons while she braided my hair, and Juan quietly stared out at the passing yellow *pampas* and blue sky.

I would learn from his little *prima* that Juan had never brought a girl out to the campo before. So when we arrived and joined twenty family members in three houses on the idyllic property, Juan and I were the subject of a lot of questions, and curious looks, and raised eyebrows. All in the friendliest, most welcoming of ways . . . which, it turns out, made Juan even tenser.

"*Lo amas?*" groups of little girls would ask me, in whispers, with secret smiles.

Do you love him?

His family did not do their part to turn me off my fantasy life as a *señora del campo*. There were walks during golden sunsets over the fields, picnics and maté and great conversation in the grass by the stream. There was a cook who spent the day rolling hundreds of gnocchi for our lunch, while her husband, the oldest of three generations of Hugos who all worked the land (Hugo, Hugito, and eight-year-old Hugitito), killed and cooked a lamb over an open fire for our dinner. There were dozens of charming kids kissing me *Buenos días* on my cheek, and sitting in my lap as I read my portion of the Stations of the Cross aloud, in Spanish, around the fire on Good Friday. Juan and the boys all played *bici polo* on the lawn while Australian shepherd dogs chased the mallet-wielding, gorgeous Argentine men in their gaucho caps. We rode horses with cushy sheepskins instead of saddles, and met Saudis who had flown in to shop for Arabian horses.

Maybe I'm not totally sure we're not supposed to end up together . . . I certainly could at least watch him ride a bike around with a polo mallet for the rest of my days.

On Easter Sunday, all twenty of us piled into cars and went into town for church. It was a tiny country *iglesia*, and held maybe a hundred people. We were all handed candles for the Light of Christ portion of the mass as we entered. Juan's older cousin, a happy, funny woman who had gone to fancy English schools in Buenos Aires and now lived on the campo with her husband and five children, handed me a candle with a special whisper:

"I know the light of Christ is not yet in your heart, but I see it in your eyes."

When it came time for everyone to take Communion, every single person in the church filed up to the front. All of the community, Juan's tiny cousins, Juan's seventy-year-old aunt and uncle. Everyone walked up to the priest holding their candles, except for me and Juan. I didn't go, obviously, because I'm not Catholic. But while everyone else in the church apparently knew why Juan didn't go either, I wouldn't find out why until later.

It was because of me. Because he had sinned since his last confession (a lot, especially in the shower; good Lord, especially in the shower) and was not worthy of receiving Communion.

I had sullied him. And now everybody in town knew.

Later that night, everyone else went to sleep, and Juan and I stayed up reading by the fire. We had been given separate rooms, but were staying alone in the house, so sexy time was certainly possible right there on the couch . . . I thought. But then I crawled onto Juan's chest, and tried to kiss him.

He didn't kiss me back.

And so we finally talked about it.

"I think you are falling in love, and I am not," Juan began.

"But you weren't!" Hope reminded me as I wept on the phone in the Panama airport.

"I know, but why wasn't he? Is it because I'm too old now? Do you think he was grossed out having sex with me all month? Do you think he wished I hadn't come? I can't believe it's over and I'm just single and alone!" I was snotty.

I learned from Juan, as I cried and we talked, that, unlike me, he had not gone into the month mostly sure it wasn't going to work out. He wouldn't have done it at all if that were how he felt. He brought me into his life for the first time because he thought maybe it *would* work.

"So, you really thought you'd maybe move to L.A., or I'd move to Buenos Aires, and we'd figure it out?" I asked.

"Well . . . yes."

I hated that conversation. The greatest thing about vacation romances is you don't have to break up, or say hard things to each other about what you are or aren't feeling. You don't have to talk about what isn't working, or why. You get to just tell yourselves that it would have lasted forever if not for the geography. *You don't have to break up.*

But Juan needed to break up. I still don't know when he realized he wasn't falling in love with me. But when he did, he became racked with guilt about the sex, and about thinking he was leading me on. Unlike me, he hadn't spent a decade learning how to be madly in love for the length of a vacation, even if he wasn't in love at all. And he wasn't on vacation—he was smack-dab in the middle of his life, where I was being warmly embraced by everyone in it, even though he knew I wasn't going to stay.

Precious little five-year-old cousins were asking him if we were going to get married, and he knew they were never going to see me again. Of course he couldn't pretend.

"*Why couldn't he just pretend?!*" I wailed to Hope from my pay phone in Panama.

"Because that's not how he works," my friend said. "You got a monthlong vacation from being single. It felt wonderful. Of course you want to be a part of that beautiful family and live in Argentina. But you and Juan aren't a match."

"I know, but now I'm just a single girl. I don't have a Same-Time-Next-Year Argentine lover anymore. I'm not going to live on a campo or have Spanish-speaking babies. It's over."

"Just come home and we'll do something fun. Maybe it's good you're putting a period on this chapter anyway. What does your mom say about voids?"

I got on my last flight home. And, once again, the plane's AV system was broken. Never fly Copa. Coming as close to a panic attack as I've ever come at the prospect of staring at the back of a seat and thinking for seven hours, I told the flight steward my story of love and loss to help him understand how badly I needed him to fix the movie situation. He seemed to share my sense of drama, and so gasped and squeezed my shoulder and told me he'd try his best, but all he was able to do was get me *The Tourist* with no audio. So I plugged into iTunes, and took a midafternoon Ambien, and drifted off watching Angelina Jolie and Johnny Depp, beautiful people in a beautiful place, speaking words that it is probably better I couldn't hear. The story you imagine is almost always better than the one with the clunky dialogue.

13

"Love Like You're About to Get Deported"

Los Angeles, California
May 2011

A few months before I went to Argentina for the last time, my writer friend Erin called me up:

"Great news. This amazing guy's wife just left him. We're going to give him a few months to recover and date a little, and then I'm setting you up. Let's say May or June."

I said that sounded great; if I was single and in Los Angeles in May, I was going to be wildly lonely and disappointed about Juan and ready to meet an amazing guy. So our timelines worked nicely.

"Great, so introduce me to my husband in May," I said glibly.

"It's on the calendar."

In May, after I returned from my last trip to Argentina, Erin introduced me to Rob. He was a writer, too, with dreamy curls, a square jaw, broad shoulders, and a big Crest smile. My boss, who writes big movies filled with nice-guy leading men you root for, recently said about him, "He's the kind of nice-guy leading man you root for in the movies." When we met, he was newly separated after a fourteen-year marriage, with two tween sons and a wounded spirit that you could barely find underneath his incredibly buoyant, optimistic heart.

I had never dated anyone with kids. Kids had always been a deal breaker, mostly because of how awful my relationship with my own stepmother had been. I knew I wouldn't be as evil as she had been to me, but I couldn't guarantee that some guy's kids wouldn't be as evil as I had been to her, either. So I avoided the possibility.

But after a few years of dating forty-year-old men who were still acting like twenty-year-olds (which, granted, was not that different from me), I was ready for someone who had done something as huge with his four decades on earth as become a father. Rob was one of those "good ones" who got snatched up, and now he was back on the market. I liked that he was a grown-up, that he knew how to commit and raise a family. And I liked how his face changed when I asked him what his kids were like.

He needed a little help remembering how to date. I taught him that if a girl offers you a ride to your car, especially if your car is less than a block away, it's an invitation to kiss her. He learned to remove after-dinner mints from his mouth *before* moving in for a first kiss.

To be fair, I wasn't much smoother. Sure, I was apparently intimidating him with my ease at drink-ordering (dads don't get to bars that often), but the first time I saw his apartment, and, specifically, the two little blue twin beds that belonged to his sons, I was out the door in less than five minutes. The sites and smells and *reality* of two little boys were overwhelming.

But then one day, after a few weeks of nervous circling and running out of doors, Rob took me sailing, and we talked about how scared we were of each other. I asked him what he thought we should do about it. His suggestion was immediate:

"I think you should sleep over."

I laughed. "Really. Like, just sleep?"

"Yes. You should just come over to my house, and stay there all night, and then we'll be used to each other and not so scared."

"So, sleep over, like, PG-style? Just jammies, movies, nothing scary, like that?"

"Yes, exactly," he lied.

I slept over. It was PG for exactly four minutes. But it worked. Very slowly, we started to grow ever so less afraid. Rob climbed Kilimanjaro with his brother later that month, and the advice from the porters on how to get to the top was a Swahili term, *polepole*. It basically means to go slowly and softly, one step at a time. Take it easy. When Rob heard the advice on that mountain in Tanzania, he thought of us. So *polepole* was our mantra.

And so that was what we were doing when my evil stepmother's boob exploded.

Really. Apparently, she had noticed a lump in her breast nine months before the tumor ruptured. She didn't tell anyone, even though her sister had come through stage three uterine cancer. She didn't have a doctor look at it, even though she worked five days a week at a hospital. She just ignored it, like, apparently, an alarming percentage of people who know they have cancer do, until, one day, in front of my dad and all of their children, the tumor grew so large that it ruptured and her breast literally burst.

They rushed her to the hospital. They did the things they do to people with breast cancer. They learned the cancer had spread to her lungs and lymph nodes. The wound from the rupture in her breast would never fully heal, and the tumor was inoperable.

And ten years into our amicable peace, I hated her again. This might not have been the kindest reaction, but a mother of four children, one of them only eleven years old, *ignored* her grapefruit-size tumor. Her horrible judgment was going to actually kill her, and to deprive the children that I loved of their mother. The *one thing* this woman had going for her, in my mind, was her youth. She would outlive my father. She'd take care of him, and take care of the kids of an elderly man. But now she wasn't even going to do that. My rage was back, all the old evil stepmother wounds freshly opened and salted.

And that's exactly when I started dating a guy with two kids.

I didn't meet Rob's sons for a long time. We wanted to be positive we were on a serious road before we involved them. *Polepole.* But we also waited because I had *very* particular rules that I thought would keep us from making the same mistakes my father had made introducing me to Patty.

First, I thought it was very important to roll out the news slowly. Because children of divorce have a *tremendous* amount of potentially terrible news to absorb, from "Mommy and Daddy are splitting up" all the way through to "Mommy and Daddy are dating, then marrying, and maybe then procreating." In my case, my father had decided to deliver all of this terrible news in one fell swoop. "I have a lover named Patty, and we're getting married because you're about to get a new brother or sister!" was his play. I was in ninth grade, and furious, and I prayed to a God I did not necessarily believe in that she would lose the baby. And then, on my fourteenth birthday, I got the news that she did. And they called off the wedding for two more years.

Do what you will with that information. I'm still sorting it.

I did not want my boyfriend's kids to summon deities to ruin my life, so I was not particularly calm. Rob, on the other hand, was very calm. He is not a child of divorce, and is also an eternal optimist. He was sure we'd all get along great!

This is, of course, why we are a good match. I am on constant alert to impending disaster, and he is constantly certain that everything is going to be okay. We developed a shorthand for discussing this difference between us, which came from something I read once about anxiety. Basically, ancient man lived to procreate another day if he was on the lookout for things that might eat him, like a bear. So, mild anxiety that there might be a bear behind that tree keeps you ready so you can escape if there is indeed a bear behind the tree. An ancient man with no anxiety often became a delicious amuse-bouche.

So when I sense impending doom, and Rob seems relaxed and calm, I say:

"Dude, bear behind the tree!"

Often, there *is* a bear behind the tree, and he's grateful I showed him, surprised that I even knew to look. Other times, he takes my hand, and makes me walk around the tree, and points out that there's no bear after all, and I calm down. It's a good combo.

We thus rolled out the new-girlfriend news at a snail's pace. In my experience, there were a ton of starving grizzlies behind this tree. I didn't love that the kids hadn't gotten any "Daddy's dating" news before the "Daddy has a girlfriend" news, and we briefly toyed with the idea of making up stories of bad dates for them to hear about for a couple of months. That had been my experience when my mom started dating, and, after hearing about enough guys breaking up with her for aerobics instructors, or having nervous breakdowns in Venezuela over another woman, I was rooting for her to find someone. But we ultimately decided that starting the whole shebang off with a lie seemed incorrect.

So he just told them about me. And they didn't cry, and wail, and beg for Daddy to go back to Mommy. They asked to see my picture, and wanted to know how we met. They said they were glad to see their newly divorced father so happy, after such a sad year. They talked about wanting to do some activity they were good at when they met me, so they could impress me.

Basically, they made me feel like an asshole. I was a terrible child.

Meanwhile, my stepmother got sicker and sicker, not responding to any of the treatments. I threw an over-the-top Christmas, with a shopping spree designed to cure cancer. Instead it just cured a lack of cashmere shawls, and scarves for balding heads.

Meanwhile, Rob and I carefully planned the kid-meeting. We handpicked activities—nothing the boys would feel insecure doing, a combination of hangout time and playtime, and then, so we could just get used to being around each other without having to talk, we'd go see a show. We settled on the Cirque du Soleil show at the Santa Monica pier, realizing later that we had fallen into the perfect stereotype—Daddy was introducing his kids to his new girlfriend by taking them to the circus. I had images of two weeping children, holding a balloon and a cotton candy and a huge stuffed bear that in no way made up for their broken home.

To avoid this, we had a set of rules, also based on things I hated as a child with dating parents. We would not touch each other in front of them. We would let the kids choose which of us they would sit by at the show. At the end of the night, Rob would not walk me out to the car. I didn't want them to wonder what he was doing down in the garage with me. I wanted them to feel like I was leaving him with them, like I was a visitor and they were the home team. I would only hug them good-bye if they hugged me. Again, a lot of worry.

My therapist says, "All tenderness comes from your first pain." That is, all of those buttons that get pushed in your life, all of the things that bother you and worry you irrationally more than the same things bother other people, they all have to do with your first big heartbreak. I could access the feelings from those early years with my stepmother like they had happened yesterday, and I was terrified of making Rob's kids feel any of them.

I met up with all of them at the beach on a sunny winter day a couple of months after they learned about me. (*Polepole!*) The oldest wanted me to see him surf, on a new board he had just bought himself. I walked across the sand, and spotted the three of them silhouetted against the sparkling ocean. One big man, two little ones. They were a flurry of happy movement, hugging, wrestling, playing. I started to laugh, and cry a little, all alone on the sand, and snapped pictures from a distance, a stepkid paparazza. Was this what my family looked like? After all of these years of looking at other happy families, was this one mine?

The kids ran up to me, and shook my hand. They answered my questions, and asked me questions, and I buried the nine-year-old in the sand. The twelve-year-old showed me his scars, and I told him that, one day, girls will flirt by asking him to tell the stories of how he got them. He liked that, and vowed to make up some good stories. They were whip smart, and hilarious, and seemed completely happy and calm.

We cleaned up and then walked to the circus, stopping on the way at the playground rings on the beach, so they could show off their tricks. I did some tricks, too, giving myself a little whiplash, and a blood blister. *Like me!!!!* At the circus, the little one switched seats, and sat next to me. It took everything I had not to touch him—he had his father's dreamy curls, and keeping my fingers out of them was an act of extreme willpower, reminding me of great first dates, where you're trying to play it cool. At the end of the night, they hugged me good-bye. I was in love.

And, the next day, I got the review: the kids had made a new Wii avatar named Kristin. A little boy home run.

Two weeks after I met the kids who will make me a stepmother, my evil stepmother died. Now, this is the happily-ever-after in Disney films. The moment that is followed by song-and-dance numbers, where happy little people and all of the creatures of the forest flutter and celebrate, and the long-tormented princess gets her prince. *Ding-dong.*

In real life, the princess, in the form of a thirty-eight-year-old, grudge-holding sitcom writer, found out via text from her eleven-year-old sister:

MY MOMMY PASSED AWAY ☹

We learned that the tumor had been growing for years.

It took a long time for it to fill her breast, because it was a very large breast. At my stepmother's funeral there were many mentions of how proud she was of the top half of her body. My stepsister, who stopped working and moved home to nurse her mother and take care of our littler siblings when her mother was diagnosed, said that her mom would often talk about her high school years in the Philippines, where she was "popular, because she was skinny with big boobs." My nineteen-year-old sister talked about how confusing her mother could be on the subject, shouting, "Don't let boys touch your boobs" at her whenever she left the house. Yet, when it came time to buy a prom dress, she would guide my sister to the dresses that were the lowest cut, with the advice, "Show more of your boobs, it's sexier!"

In Greece, it is bad luck to compliment the beauty of a new baby, because there is a superstition that it will attract the negative attention of the Gods. So, like an actor is told to "break a leg," new parents in Greece hear, "What an ugly baby!" That was what I was thinking about as I listened to Patty's sisters and daughters talk about her obsession with the exact body part that ended up killing her.

I did not plan on speaking at my stepmother's funeral. I thought I had nothing nice to say. I thought that everyone would see the truth: that my heart was breaking for my motherless little siblings, but that *I was not grieving*. Because maybe my father now had a chance for a fresh start from a woman he could not afford to divorce. Maybe he would even sober up now that he wasn't in an unhappy marriage, and do yard work again, and get off the couch and engage in the world like he used to and be the kind of father to my baby sister he had been to me before it all went so, so wrong. Maybe he would finally be *happy*. I was afraid everyone would see that even though Patty and I had, finally, exchanged "I love you"s, and I had prayed to the God I once invoked to hurt her to this time make her better, that *I wouldn't miss her.*

But then my siblings spoke.

And they were eloquent, and beautiful. I was so *proud* of these people that Patty had made. They told us all things I had never known about their mother, and spoke about her in ways that made me wonder if I would have hated her so much if she hadn't been cast as the Bad Guy in the movie of my life. Then they led us all in an Our Father, a prayer I only knew because I had said it at a tremendous number of other people's weddings:

"Forgive us our trespasses, as we forgive those who trespass against us."

I had spent the week watching my siblings sleep in one room, piled on and around each other for support, just like their family-centric mom had taught them to do. And I realized that, someday, when my own mom dies, and when our dad dies, I'll have them just like they have each other. If it weren't for my stepmother, I would have had to go through that alone. Instead, I'll probably go through it in a bed filled with people and dogs and cats and snacks. And, so, I stood up, and I thanked Patty for giving me the greatest gift of my life.

And I wondered if she might not have been so awful if I had been as kind to her as my boyfriend's kids were being to me.

———————

Vacation romances are so sweet because they're finite. *Every* moment together is one of your last. They're the one bite of dessert you're allowed on your big diet, the fifteen-minute nap stolen by an exhausted new parent. The world is a thing that exists only to tear the two of you apart, which brings you very close together. And the fact that you found each other at all, on this huge planet, in this Bedouin cave or that boat in the middle of the Great Barrier Reef, feels like a *miracle*.

But regular relationships are going to end, too... even if it's when you're a hundred years old. Furthermore, *life* is going to end. (I'm tempted to say, "Life is going to end, *man*," because my reference to mortality makes me feel ridiculous. But it is, man.) And if you can somehow remember that all of life, and every relationship, is going to end, man, *every* moment becomes sweet. *Every* kiss *could* be your last, even thirty years into a marriage, even if you marry a much younger spouse who is supposed to outlive you, even if you Settle for Mr. Good Enough who you're sure will never leave you, even if you wait for Mr. Movie Moment. It's all as fleeting as a once-in-a-lifetime weekend on an exotic island. The challenge is to hold on to that.

The summer after losing her mom, my baby sister came out to L.A. and went to summer camp with Rob's boys, who are about her age. Rob's oldest son pointed out that if Rob married me and he married my (adorable) sister, he and his father would be brothers-in-law. Which will most probably end up a TV pilot. Watching my sister and Rob's sons play together felt like the happy ending to so many sad divorces, so many splintered families. The pieces were finally re-forming into something new.

Am I still terrified of settling down? Of course. But I think it's going to go okay. Last week I had a Saturday-night family dinner with the three boys. I picked up dessert, which has become my thing. Rob had just had a work triumph, and so I also brought a bottle of champagne, and a bottle of Martinelli's. He wasn't sure if he'd gotten the champagne flutes in the divorce, but we found them, buried deep in a high cabinet. We blew dust out of the flutes, and poured four glasses of bubbles.

After dinner, we decided to play Wii. The kids turned on the game, and dozens of avatars they had created ran around on the screen. There I was, the little me they had made, and I wasn't fat or old, like I had feared. I looked a lot like me. A little version of their dad was there, too, and both kids, and both sets of grandparents, and the kids' mom. All of us running around on the same screen now, together.

I ran this book by Rob before I sold it (making him read this last chapter first; I'm no dummy). I wanted to make sure he was okay with it for obvious bleeding-on-Brazilian reasons. After settling down with a couple of stiff drinks and the manuscript, he reassuringly offered me his complete support. And then this:

"You inspired me," he said. "I'm kind of jealous of all your adventures."

Oh shit. The *last* person I want getting inspired to run off and have sexy single international adventures is him. But then he continued:

"I think before we have another kid, I want to have been on all seven continents with you."

I told my mom about this perfect ending that he gave me, for my life, and for my book. Our girl doesn't have to stay home to find love and family, she has to hit the road again, but now with one to three extra boys in tow!

"Hm, interesting," my mother said.

One week later, she called with an offer she had never before made: for my Christmas present, she wanted to buy Rob and me a trip.

"Anywhere in the world Rob has never been," was my mother's only stipulation for her attempt to purchase a grandchild.

This spring we hit Asia and South America, trips that incredibly poetically filled up the last page of the single-girl passport I got for that first trip to Argentina. That passport features a photo of a shiny, bleary-eyed, thirty-year-old girl who had rushed to the last-minute passport desk after a sleepless night spent tussling with a young punk rocker. It replaced the passport with the photo of the pudgy-cheeked college senior about to go to Europe with her first boyfriend for the first time. Both of them are now in a hidden drawer with my grandma's jewelry, the place where I keep my most valuable possessions.

I'd tell you the stories from my first trip out of the country with a boyfriend in almost fifteen years . . . but they're personal. I will say that it was *really* nice to be flying back to Los Angeles free of the debilitating realization that I had to get back on Match.com when I got home. And I will say that all Rob has left is Antarctica.

"Surely he's not going to hold you to Antarctica," my mother said.

Epilogue

....

"Awesome for Awesome"

In perfect-movie-ending timing, as I write this last chapter of a book about my single life, I'm living the last week of my single life. Rob and I bought a house together in Santa Monica for the four of us and my cat and his sons' dog, and we're moving in next week, the same week my book is due. So I'm sorting through closets filled with decades of old love letters and pictures and plane tickets, old money belts filled with lists of long-gone clubs in Amsterdam and international phone numbers and travelers check receipts (remember those?). I'm putting them all away into boxes as I run back and forth to my computer putting away memories into this book. The book can go on a shelf in our new house, the boxes might have to go into deep storage. But they're both getting put away.

I found a renter for the single-girl house that I bought nine years ago, the house I thought I'd only be in for a couple of years before finding my guy. A hilarious comedienne is moving in, using it as her landing pad after a divorce. It makes me happy that someone who makes me laugh is going to lick her wounds in the house that kept me warm and safe while I licked mine.

I've been walking around my neighborhood taking pictures—of the baristas who helped me learn how to have Sunday breakfast alone, of my favorite Banksy mural of cats running across a wall down the block. I'm only moving eight miles away, but I'm saying good-bye to this place like it's an exotic, beloved foreign land that I may never see again. I'm *really* sad about leaving my house, and my life. But how lucky is that? It means despite the lonely moments, the nights in bed saying "I love you" to no one just because it had been so long since I had said "I love you" before going to sleep, that I was happy here. Even though this book was all about my struggle to NOT be a sad, single girl looking for love, that does not mean I was not often a sad, single girl, and I was absolutely looking for love. I just thought love was going to look different than it turned out to look, and so I ran away from it a lot. But my story wasn't ultimately a sad story. Being a single girl was pretty spectacular. Thank God I'm blue about changing my life. It means I'm trading awesome for awesome.

I don't think I would have published this book if I were still single. I would have been afraid it would be too much for someone who was considering dating me. Even though I was comfortable in my skin as a single woman, and I'm proud of the life I've lived, I wouldn't have felt comfortable enough to do something as naked as write this all down if I was still looking for love. Shockingly (to maybe only me), being in a relationship has done the opposite of limiting me. It's emboldened me to try something much scarier than I would have tried if I were alone. Maybe Rachel the Hasidic journalist was right: love frees you to be the person you actually are.

My ending up with a nice guy with two kids in my own town is as much of a miracle as it would have been for me to end up with a priest from Argentina. It took an *awful* lot of running to and from so many things to turn into the person who would make this choice. My nice guy may live in my city, but I had to travel farther to find him than I had to travel to find Father Juan or Aleg or Inon or Cristiano. It was a long trip . . . but a great one.

So, finally, *finally*, I didn't choose a bite of decadent dessert that leaves you hungry, and a little sick, and disappointed in yourself for the poor care you are taking of your body. I've finally chosen a healthy, delicious, three-course meal. But if there is one message I want to put out into the world with my little life story, it's this: It's also okay to sometimes have popcorn and red wine for dinner. It's a harmless kind of naughty that can make a night alone on the couch a lot of fun.

Also, get on a plane by yourself and go have an adventure. I know I still will.

So, now that you know the whole story, here, finally, is my last dedication:

> *And to my guy,*
>
> *who gave me my last chapter,*
>
> *and the final stamp in my single-girl passport.*
>
> *Sorry I'll look so old in the photo for my new one.*
>
> *(That last one took longer to fill than I expected.)*

About the Author

KRISTIN NEWMAN is a television writer who has worked in Hollywood for nearly twenty years. She has written for *That '70s Show, Chuck, How I Met Your Mother,* and *The Neighbors.* Please visit her on Tumblr at TheOtherKristinNewman.tumblr.com and Twitter at twitter.com/TheOtherKristin.